WEEKEND**escape**

AMSTERDAM

A great weekend
in Amsterdam

Wherever you are in Europe, you're never more than an hour or so away from Amsterdam by plane, so there's no excuse for not spending a few days in the city they call the "Venice of the North," the "city of tulips," the "city of a hundred canals," the "diamond capital" or the "city of the golden century." But, clichés aside, Amsterdam is like nowhere else on earth. Famed for its cheese, its tulips, its canals and its art museums, Amsterdam has something for everyone. The city's many faces are as varied as its districts which, though closely packed together, are all quite unique.

Amsterdam is a paradoxical place, conservative in some ways, pioneering in many others. This home of right-thinking Calvinists was the first city to establish a trade union for prostitutes, pass draconian laws against pollution from cars and legalize marriage between people of the same sex. Amsterdam's coffee-shops, where the sale and consumption of cannabis is permitted, and its highly mixed and apparently mutually accepting population of 145 different nationalities reflect the city's tolerant attitudes. If there's one thing all Amsterdammers share, it's a love of trade, which sends them traveling all over the world to bring back the rare objects you find in the big antique shops on

Spiegelstraat or the Rokin. But the city also has dozens of junk shops, which are fun to explore and also have some real bargains. Take advantage of your trip to buy all your garden bulbs or hunt down the last word in gadgets in the Jordaan district. You can buy cheap clothes here too, as long as you're not expecting the elegance of Paris or Milan.

With only 730,000 inhabitants – and 550,000 bicycles – Amsterdam is still a small city, enclosed by a network of canals linked to the North Sea. You can easily get around it on foot, among the patrician houses and numerous cafés, losing yourself in places that resemble a Van Goyen seascape

or a genre painting by Jan Steen. It's then that you

begin to understand why Amsterdammers use the word *gezellig* so often. This is an untranslatable word that's often used to convey the conviviality of their relaxed surroundings. It doesn't take long before Amsterdam's love of partying turns the streets into a color carnival full of crazy outfits, pointed hats, purple-haired punks and young men swathed in leather. After you've watched one of these spontaneous shows, spent time admiring Rembrandt's painting of *The Night Watch* and Van Gogh's *Sunflowers*

and are at last leaning on the counter of one of the city's 1,402 cafés or dancing under a club's hypnotic lights, you'll know you've touched the beating heart of Amsterdam. Having glimpsed its true face, stammered out a few words in Dutch, tasted some of the thousand subtle flavors of *jenever*, watched one of the forty shows on offer every day of the week, rifled through all the market stalls and been to every museum in town, you'll know that there's only one thing left for you to do, and that's come back to Amsterdam.

How to get there

The best season

Spring and summer are probably the best seasons in which to get the most out of your weekend trip to Amsterdam, but you can never be absolutely certain of getting the better of the Dutch climate.

In practice, it may be rainy and cold at any time of year. July and August are not only the hottest months (21-26°C/ 70-79°F), they're also the period when most hotels charge low season prices. And if you can cope with bitterly cold, damp weather,

Amsterdam is quite charming in the depths of winter, when the frozen canals bring to mind the works of the great 17th-century painters.

How to get here

Since cars are completely useless in Amsterdam, the quickest and most comfortable way to travel is by plane. But if Amsterdam is part of a European tour, you may like to try the fast Thalys train. This train will take you from the center of Paris to the center of Amsterdam in just over four hours. You can also take the Eurostar from London (see box p. 5).

By plane

Amsterdam is a major European gateway and airlines periodically offer amazing deals that bring the price of a

return ticket to significantly less than the price of a train or other overland journey. The permitted maximum allowance for luggage taken in the hold is 23kg/50lbs in economy class and 30kg/66lbs in business class. If you go over the limit you'll have to pay a surcharge calculated by weight.

FROM THE UK
Among the major carriers flying to Schiphol airport from the UK are:

British Airways
www.british-airways.com
☎ 0870 850 9850
Frequent daily direct flights from the UK to Amsterdam.

British Midland
www.flybmi.com
☎ 0870 6070 555
Up to eight daily flights to Amsterdam from the UK.

Easyjet
www.easyjet.com
☎ 0870 6000 000
Regular daily flights from UK airports.

KLM
www.klm.com
☎ 08705 074 074
Regular flights to Amsterdam from 15 UK airports.

ARRIVING BY TRAIN

If you'd prefer to travel by train, Amsterdam is only a few hours away from any major city in mainland Europe on the high-speed Thalys service, run by the French, Belgian, German and Dutch railways. You can book online on www.thalys.com.

The Eurostar offers a fast service direct from London to Brussels or Paris where you can transfer to trains for Amsterdam. For more information log on to their websites:
www.eurostar.com
☎ 08705 186 186
www.raileurope.co.uk
☎ 08705 848 84.

FROM THE US/CANADA

KLM/Northwest
www.klm.com / www.nwa.com
☎ 0800 447 4747
Daily code-shared services from major airports.

Delta
www.delta-air.com
☎ 0900 525 0280
Daily flights direct to Amsterdam from major airports.

United Airlines
☎ 0800 242 4444
www.united.com
Flies to Amsterdam from Chicago and Washington.

Air Canada
www.aircanada.com
☎ 888 247 2262
Flies to Amsterdam via London.

Many other flights include a European stopover.

FROM AUSTRALIA/NEW ZEALAND
The Dutch airline KLM flies direct to Amsterdam from Sydney, but it may be cheaper to find a flight with a stopover. From New Zealand, you can fly with Qantas via Sydney, and KLM offers a code share with Air New Zealand to Amsterdam via Los Angeles. All major airlines fly to Europe, and it's worth seeing a travel agent to work out the cheapest and most convenient route.

KLM
www.klm.com
☎ 02 9922 1555 (Australia)
☎ 09 309 1782
(New Zealand)

Qantas
www.qantas.com
☎ 13 12 11 or 02 9261 3636
(Australia)

INCLUSIVE BREAKS

Many tour operators offer two- or three-day weekend breaks at fixed prices which include transport and accommodation. Some of the best deals can be found in the travel sections of the weekend newspapers, or your local travel agent should be able to assist you.
The Amsterdam Travel Service (☎ 0870 727 5972 www.amsterdamtravel.co.uk) can plan and organize your entire itinerary for you. You could also check current deals on the internet with websites such as Expedia (www.expedia.com), Travelocity (www.travelocity.com) or the Travel Shop (www.traveleshop.com).

☎ 09 357 8900 or
0800 808 967 (New Zealand)
Qantas flies daily from Sydney
to Amsterdam, usually via
London and an Asian airport.
All flights from New Zealand
go via Sydney.

British Airways

www.british-airways.com
☎ 02 9258 3300 (Australia)
☎ 09 356 8690
(New Zealand)
British Airways offers daily
flights from Sydney and other
Australian cities, via London
Heathrow.

From the airport to the center

Schiphol airport is 18km
(11 miles) southwest of
Amsterdam. You have a choice
of three modes of transport to
take you to the city center.
Quickest and fastest is the

train, which gets you to
Amsterdam's central station in
20 mins. Departures every
10 mins until 12.30am and
every hour between 1am and
6am, from the airport station
located under the terminal.
Ticket offices are open day
and night (€3.20 one-way;
€5.70 round-trip). A
Connexxion bus to six of
Amsterdam's major hotels
leaves the airport's main exit
every half hour between
6.30am and 6pm. Buy
your ticket from the driver,
price €11. You can get a

VOLTAGE & TIME

In the Netherlands the
electricity supply is 220
volts. The plugs are
round two-pin, and you
will probably need to
bring an adapter.
Amsterdam summer
time is two hours ahead
of GMT; winter time is
GMT + one hour.

taxi from the airport direct
to your hotel door for about
€39. Journey time varies
from 30 mins to 1 hour.

Amsterdam by car

Unless you're intending to
tour the country around
Amsterdam, a car will just be a
source of problems. There are
very few hotels with a free car
park and you'll spend a
fortune on parking meters
(€3.20 per hour) if you want
to avoid getting your car
clamped (costing you at least
€69 to remove). The city is
comparatively small and
public transport runs all night
so you're really better off
leaving the car at home.
However, if you can't bear to
be without your own wheels
and are at least 21 years old,
you'll be better off renting a
car. You can arrange this from
home, otherwise the car rental
offices at Schiphol (open from

THE *TREINTAXI*

To get from the station to your hotel, you can take the shared *treintaxi* that leave approximately every ten minutes. The tickets (€4) are sold in automatic ticket machines in the station. To reserve a *treintaxi* to take you to your hotel call:
☎ 900 87 34 68 82 or www.treintaxi.nl

6am to 10.30pm) are in Schiphol Plaza in the Arrivals lounge, before customs. Europcar offers the best weekend rates, but you may need to reserve in advance:
☎ 0 825 352 352
www.europcar.co.uk

When you arrive in Amsterdam, follow the signs for P+R Transférium, which will lead you to the best supervised and most economic parking in the city center. For prices and maps see the website: www.naaramsterdam.nl.

To arrange to have a clamp removed or buy a daily parking ticket (€25.20):
Stadstoezicht
Several addresses in Amsterdam
Mon.-Fri. 8am-6pm,
Sat. 8am-3.30pm.
Bureau Central
Daniël Goedkoopstraat, 7
☎ 553 03 33
Every day, 24 hours.

Entry procedures

EU citizens should carry a valid ID card or passport. Non-EU citizens will require a valid passport, although US citizens do not require a visa to enter the Netherlands. No vaccinations are necessary.

Customs

For travelers returning to other EU countries, there are few restrictions on alcohol or tobacco products. The only stipulation is that the goods must be for personal use and guidelines are provided, for example 10 liters of spirits, 90 liters of wine and 800 cigarettes. Duty-free limits for travelers leaving the EU are as follows:
Alcohol over 22%: 1 liter *or* alcohol under 22%: 2 liters *and* still table wine: 2 liters.
Cigarettes: 200 *or* cigars: 50 *or* tobacco, 250gm.
Perfume: 60ml.
Toilet water: 250ml.
If you're taking your dog or cat, don't forget to bring a vaccination certificate verified by your vet 30 days before departure.

Insurance and health

If you pay for your ticket by credit card, you automatically benefit from some insurance regarding your luggage, the possible cancelation of your trip and medical repatriation. Find out more from your credit card company or ask your bank. EU citizens can also reclaim medical expenses once back home; make sure you take a European Health Insurance Card (forms available from post offices). Non-EU citizens should make

sure they have adequate cover. The cost is low but it offers real benefits in case of problems.

If you're following a special course of medical treatment, make sure you take enough medication with you to cover the time you'll be away, as you can't be sure of finding it in Amsterdam. You'll discover numerous very well-stocked chemist's shops in Amsterdam selling everything from toothpaste and hair-care products to sun-screen, vitamins, food supplements and some medicinal items that you might normally only expect to obtain on prescription back home.

Currency

On January 1, 2002 the euro (€) replaced the official currency of 12 European nations, including the Netherlands, and the guilder ceased to be legal tender at midnight on January 28 2002. The euro is divided into 100 cents. The convenience of the euro means you no longer have to change money when traveling between the 12 states. You can buy traveler's checks in euros and change them in Amsterdam, Brussels or Paris, although you will be charged a handling fee. Credit and debit cards work normally and your account will be debited by the dollar or sterling equivalent of the euro on your transaction slip. You should make sure you retain your transaction slip to compare with your account statement, to ensure that the currency conversion was correct.

There are plenty of cash machines in the city and at the airport, and you can easily withdraw cash using a credit or banker's card. If you need to carry large sums of money around with you, it's better to take traveler's checks as pickpocketing is known to be rife in the city.

All major credit cards are recognized in the Netherlands and most large shops and restaurants will take cards in payment. However, you should still ensure that you're not caught short without enough cash to cover your daily expenses. Car rental agencies will usually wish to see a credit card. Some shops will charge a 5 percent surcharge on credit card payments. Travelers resident in non-EU countries can claim back the value added tax (BTW) if they spend above a certain amount in a single visit to a shop. Check with customs, or look out for shops advertising tax-free shopping for overseas tourists.

Budgeting

Living in Amsterdam is expensive. It costs from €18 to €45 for a meal, from €4 to €11 for entrance to a museum, €1.60 for a tram ticket, €1.50 to €4 for a coffee or beer, €7 to €15 to get into a disco, and €10 to €25 for a theater or concert seat. On top of costs for transport and accommodation for the weekend (€500 to €750), you need to allow €400 to €600 for spending money.

Of course, if you're traveling on a student budget, Amsterdam is still very much within your reach: you can get something to eat and a place to stay for very little, although the conditions can only be described as somewhat spartan. But however much you have to spend, the enormous choice of hotels and restaurants means that you'll always be able to find a room and a meal to suit your pocket.

Amsterdam is a city of diamonds, antiques, books and curiosities, so if you're looking to buy any of these, you'll find there are some very good bargains to be had. Many gadgets, items for the home, ready-to-wear clothes and accessories are attractively priced and you'll often find items here that you can't get elsewhere. Generally speaking, Dutch fashions tend to follow the broad trends of other European countries and you'll find a range of synthetic materials rather than natural linens and raw silk.

Queen's Day

If you're planning to go to Amsterdam at the end of April, you'll need to reserve your hotel a long way in advance. April 30 is Queen's Day (see p. 33), when every town in the Netherlands is buzzing and people fill the streets to celebrate the queen's birthday. The actual festivities take place either the weekend before or after April 30.

Frans Hals, The Archers' Banquet

Jean Calvin, 16th-century
wood engraving

Reflections
of the Golden Age

In the 17th century Amsterdam became one of Europe's most flourishing capitals, thanks to the success of its traders and the freedom of thought permitted in the city. The Dutch welcomed exiles from all sides and in ten years the city had doubled in size. Meanwhile, the wealthy merchants of the prestigious Dutch East India Company were challenging the Portuguese monopoly of the spice trade.

engaged in trading goods, everyone is so occupied attending to his profit that I could stay here for the rest of my life without ever being seen by anyone."
René Descartes, 1631.

The Calvinist creed

"Let us take the gain that comes to us as though it were from the hand of God." With advice like that John Calvin was bound to appeal to the merchants of Amsterdam, who abandoned the teachings of the Spanish Catholics and welcomed many refugees, guaranteeing them both economic freedom and the freedom to think and worship as they chose.

Economic and religious liberalism

The vast influx of foreign capital made it possible to fund major maritime expeditions and also to develop local industries, such as brewing, silk manufacture, diamond-cutting, printing, map-making and ship-building.
"In this great city where, other than myself, there is not a single man who is not

A city without palaces

The only aim the rich Calvinists had in making money was to hoard their wealth. They were not interested in ostentatious splendor, or palaces, so there's no architecture worthy of the Golden Age. All you'll find are a few decorative masks and grotesque figures to enliven the modest gabled brick façades. Given that tax was assessed by the *"kavel,"* or plot of building land with a width of 7.35m (8yds) and a depth of 60m (65yds), few people risked building on much larger plots.

Early town planning

To house a population that had tripled in forty years, it was decided to enlarge the city by the excavation of three new canals, the Herengracht, the Keizersgracht and the Prinsengracht, around the port and the old quarters. The city was built all in one go and owes its

Gerrit Dou, Woman with Dropsy

harmonious quality to the rules imposed by the local council, which specified not only what materials could be used and the dimensions of the houses, but also located their inhabitants according to their social status, work or origins.

The birth of bourgeois art

Freed from the yoke of religion, Dutch painters diversified into genres which reveal the material concerns of their wealthy bourgeois patrons. Commissions for single and group portraits came flooding into the studios of well-known painters such as Rembrandt and Frans Hals. Pictures of landscapes or simple church interiors were successful in a way unheard-of elsewhere. However, these highly realistic depictions express a strict Protestant morality – tavern scenes portray the evils of excessive alcohol and tobacco consumption while the withered flowers of the still lifes are reminders of the vanity of worldly wealth and pleasures.

A DIFFERENT IMAGE OF REMBRANDT

Rembrandt van Rijn's real name was Rembrandt Harmenszoon, which means "Rembrandt, son of Harmen." He married in 1634, but then took his children's nanny as his mistress. However, in 1649 she left him and took him to court for breaking his promise to marry her. The painter then took on a young serving girl, Hendrickje Stoffels, who became his companion. However, his behavior was considered scandalous because Rembrandt's fame was such that he was regarded as a public figure. The Dutch Reformed Church condemned and reprimanded him and the unfortunate Hendrickje was banned from taking Communion. The puritanical public turned against the artist, who later died in disgrace.

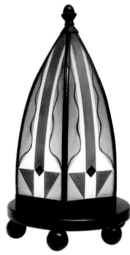

The seeds
of modernism

Turning its back on the floral exuberance of art nouveau, which was all the rage in France and Belgium, the Netherlands favored a more rational form of architecture, exploiting the potential of emerging industrial techniques. The priority in Amsterdam was to use objects and furniture as a way of bringing art into daily life. In this way the modern look came into being.

The new aesthetic creed

The "Arts and Crafts" exhibition held in London in 1880 marked the dawn of a new aesthetics which was to have an important influence on Dutch artists, particularly since the Netherlands' Germanic culture tends to favor severity over excess. The cult of the pure line and geometrical shapes acted as the vehicle of a new art form which gradually evolved towards expressionism.

Functionalism

H. P. Berlage was an important figure of the avant-garde due to the way he exploited the qualities of old and new materials in functional ways. His monumental building for the Amsterdam stock exchange (1898-1903) consisted of a simple, sober structure of glass and steel, without any form of ornamentation, standing on a structure made from brick and stone.

The Amsterdam School

The socialist city council built affordable housing in south Amsterdam for the new working class. Rationalism and progress were the watchwords. However, the "Dageraad" complex, designed between 1921 and 1923 by Michael de Klerk and P. L. Kramer, seems more fantastical than rational in conception. Expressionist ideas of movement are rather playfully reflected in the undulations, abrupt vertical constructions and the interplay of different colors.

The De Stijl movement

Founded in Leiden in 1917 by Theo van Doesburg, the De Stijl movement, whose best representative is Piet Mondrian, evolved out of neo-Plasticism. This was a theory of painting characterized by the rigorous use of very simple means of expression, such as horizontal and vertical lines, in combination with evenly applied primary colors. Sometimes black and white would also be included, either as pure colors or mixed.

A pioneer of abstract art

Mondrian, whose early influences were Toorop and Seurat, is regarded as one of the pioneers of abstract art. He made a profound impression on all of contemporary Western art, both through his pictures (*Composition in Red, Yellow and Blue* and *Victory Boogie-Woogie*, among others) and his writings, such as the

De Stijl Manifesto, The Triptych of Evolution and *Natural Reality and Abstract Reality.*

Modernism and daily life

The rigorously orthogonal forms he gave to his creations link Gerrit Rietveld (1888-1964) firmly to the De Stijl movement. The famous red and blue armchair, which he designed in 1919, marks the beginning of the era of simple furniture which could be mass-produced. Later he developed evermore purified forms, which have influenced the work of many of today's designers.

Art Deco

This catch-all term, first used during the 1925 Paris International Exhibition, covers the very varied artistic production of the first half of the 20th century. The furniture and objects made from 1915 onwards reflect a return to styles from the past, with massive forms, contrasting colors, geometrical decoration and the use of glass and steel. The use of rare materials (lacquer, leather, ivory) made this a luxury style of limited production. The category of art deco covers both Rietveld's cubist table and the comfortable "Vanity Fair" armchair.

ROBERT DUSARDUYN

This former theater designer has specialized in collecting art deco objects and furniture since 1972. His collection of velvets from the Amsterdam School is well worth a look.

Molsteeg, 5 and 7
☎ 623 21 89
Fri. 12.30-6pm, Sat. 11.30am-6pm or by appointment.

Liberty
and libertines

Since the 17th century, Amsterdam has been known for its tolerance. Though their apparently lax attitudes have often been criticized by their European neighbors, the Dutch uphold the right to true freedom of action and thought. Differences are accepted, whether a person is foreign, gay or rejects moral conventions. Holland was also first to legalize abortion, allow euthanasia and decriminalize soft drugs.

Squatting, an outdated phenomenon

In the early 1970s it was fairly easy for a student to find free accommodation in a magnificent residence on the Herengracht. The Provos' (see p. 15) action to combat property speculation was more or less permitted by the city council, which preferred to see such buildings occupied before renovation. In what can only be seen as a sign of the times, the new housing law passed in 1986 put an end to this practice.

The Provos, gentle activists

In 1964 a group of young protesters describing themselves as nonviolent ecologists campaigning against the status quo launched a series of amusing stunts known as "happenings." They met at the Dam and advocated nonpolluting cars, the right to social housing and sexual freedom. These gentle subversives succeeded in getting elected on to the city council, where they instigated the anti-car policies in force today.

Coffee-shops and cannabis

The cannabis culture in the Netherlands was set in motion by Kees Hockert who, in 1961, discovered a loophole in Dutch law that made it illegal to possess dried cannabis flowers but not to grow them. Although the possession of soft drugs is still a crime in the Netherlands, the Dutch government permits the sale of cannabis resin in Amsterdam's 300 or so coffee-shops. However, the amount allowed for sale was recently reduced from 30gm (1oz) to 5gm (0.2oz).

Business and the limits of permissiveness

Recently the council of Delfzijl, a small town on the northern coast of the Netherlands, not far from Groningen, closed down all the local coffee-shops and opened a new one, which is run by a council employee. Not a bad way to keep a discreet eye on the customers and help balance the budget!

Love in a shop window

Like any other port, Amsterdam has its prostitutes. The difference is that here there's none of the hypocrisy to be found in other countries – the prostitutes are on display in shop windows.

Brothels are officially licensed and the women pay tax. It's a natural way of recognizing their profession and preventing them from touting for business on the streets, a practice which is still illegal in the country.

Gay city

After San Francisco, Amsterdam is the city with the highest number of gay clubs and bars in the world. It's one of the few countries in Europe where homosexual couples can marry and where they have the right to raise children. The gay community has a newspaper called the *Gay Krant*, and a center for the protection of its rights. It also has an official 'pink day' in the holiday calendar.

A COUNTRY THAT WELCOMES FOREIGNERS

A quarter of the population is non-native and 145 nationalities live side-by-side in Amsterdam. Most are from Surinam, descendants of the black African slaves who were "imported" to the Guyanas. In response to their desire to settle permanently in the Netherlands, an office was set up to help them to integrate into Dutch society. *'In what other country can one enjoy such complete freedom, can one sleep with fewer worries?'* René Descartes, 1631.

Pottery

Among the precious cargoes brought back from the East by the ships of the Dutch East India Company was the famous blue-and-white porcelain from China. The first auction in 1604 caused enormous excitement among the Dutch bourgeoisie, whose dream it was to own such treasures. Chinese porcelain was expensive because of its rarity and was soon copied in the factories of Delft, which doubled in number between 1651 and 1665.

A technique from Italy

The use of faïence was introduced to the Netherlands in the early 16th century by Italian potters who had established workshops in Antwerp. At this time kitchen equipment for daily use was made either of tin, wood or leather, following Germanic tradition. Politico-religious conflicts drove the Italian potters to migrate to the northern provinces, where they founded factories in Delft, Makkum, The Hague and Haarlem.

Delft faïence

The terms porcelain and faïence are often confused. In fact, although the factories of

Delft and Makkum began to concentrate on producing copies of Chinese porcelain in 1613, Dutch factories have never made anything but white faïence, decorated either in monochrome blue or a combination of colors. White Delftware pieces intended for kitchen use haven't been made for a very long time and are highly sought-after.

Porcelain or faïence?

In porcelain fired at high temperatures (1,350°C/2,880°F),

the china clay (kaolin) and the glaze form a flawless and highly resistant amalgam. While porcelain is very thin and translucent, faïence is made from a different kind of clay and is fired twice. After the first firing the earthenware object is covered in an opaque, white, tin-based enamel, and may be decorated. The piece is then fired again at 800°C (1,470°F). Faïence is less solid than porcelain and may also have flaws, such as bubbles caused by firing at too high a temperature or the seeping of the decoration into the enamel. Delft faïence has a second coating (transparent glaze), which heightens the colors. And in case you were wondering, the word "faïence" comes from the name of the Italian town of Faenza, where this technique was developed in the 15th century.

The blue monochrome or multicolored decoration is always hand-painted by skilled craftspeople and is more delicate than that of Delft.

De Porceleyne Fles

Most of the Delft factories closed their doors around 1742 as a result of competition from English and French products. The only factory to have maintained continuous production since it was founded in 1653 is the "De Porceleyne Fles" factory. King Willem III gave it the title of royal factory in order to stimulate its declining output. Today, this and the Makkum factory are the only ones to produce real Delftware, which is authenticated by a mark on the underside of the object.

Makkum faïence

Though less well-known by the general public, the royal factory at Makkum is the oldest in the Netherlands. It was founded in 1594 and since 1674 has been owned by the same family, the Tichelaars, who, from generation to generation, have passed down the secrets of the enamels that give the factory pieces their particular beauty.

HOW TO RECOGNIZE REAL DELFTWARE

Beware! Not all blue-and-white ceramics are Delftware. Some souvenir-sellers have no scruples in inscribing the bottom of cheap imported ceramics with the royal crown and the magic words Köninklijk Delftsblauw. The first clue to the authenticity is the price. To be certain, however, buy your Delftware from specialist shops, particularly if you're looking for antique pieces, and always check that they have the proper mark.

The tulip,
a national emblem

From the end of April, for eight or nine weeks, the polder between Leiden and Haarlem is transformed into a multicolored carpet by its 8,000ha/20,000 acres planted with tulips. This wild flower from the steppes of central Asia, which first bloomed in Holland in 1594, aroused such a passion that growers have continued to modify its shapes and colors to this day.

Flower of sultans

In the 16th century the ambassador of Ferdinand I of Austria to the court of the Ottoman sultan was surprised at the general passion for a flower then unknown in Europe – the tulip. He brought back a few bulbs, which were planted in the Imperial gardens in Vienna in 1554. Although the Turkish word for tulip is *"lale,"* the ambassador misunderstood his interpreter's description of the flower as resembling a turban (*tulband*), and thought this was in fact its name. In Latin it became known as *tulipa.*

The taming of the tulip

A French botanist, Charles de Lécluse, who was interested in the form and structure of the tulip, discovered its fantastic

capacity for hybridisation. He created the first blooms of *Tulipa gesneriana* in the Leiden botanical gardens in 1594. Little did he realize, when he made his research public, that he was unleashing a kind of madness that was to seize hold of the entire Dutch nation.

Tulips in art

The tulip, precious as a silver dish or a cut-crystal glass, became an element in the composition of still lifes. The Flemish painter Jan Breughel (1568-1625) was the first to depict it in all its ephemeral splendor. The Delft potters dedicated a special vase to the tulip, specifically designed to show off all its beauty to the greatest effect.

Tulipomania

The tulip's great success as a curiosity stimulated the greed of the speculators. All kinds of people began to experiment with the aim of obtaining a flower of rare shape or color. In 1634, the tulip was even quoted on the stock exchange and had its own lawyers to take care of transactions. The craze lasted for three years, during which time tulips were bought and sold for astronomical sums. *Semper Augustus* traded for between 4,000 and 5,500 Florins. All this speculation came to an end when the market crashed, though the

tulip remained a luxury item for a very long time afterwards.

Bulb cultivation

The Haarlem region saw an extraordinary boom in the cultivation of bulbs, which became one of the region's main exports, due to its sandy soil, rich in limestone, which is particularly suited to growing

tulips. Shortly after flowering the blooms are cut in such a way as to preserve the nutritional reserves of the bulb. These are harvested three months after the plant is cut back and go for forcing (greenhouse growing) or are stored at a variable temperature for garden planting.

"CULTIVARS"

Starting from the hundred or so tulip species to be found growing wild in central Asia, horticulturalists have developed around 900 tulip varieties, or "cultivars."
These fall into three categories, early, mid-season or late, according to the period in the year when they flower.

How to grow your tulip

Tulip bulbs should be planted between September and early December Plant your bulbs 10cm (4in) deep, whatever type of soil you have, and leave a space between them measuring roughly 15-20cm (6-8in). Depending on their variety and size, your tulips will bloom either in March or April (for early varieties) or May (for later varieties).

Tobacco
mania

In the 16th century a new craze hit Europe: the sniffing or smoking of the leaves of a plant discovered by Christopher Columbus among the American Indians. This luxury product, precious and rare, couldn't fail to interest the Dutch speculators, who set about acclimatizing the plant in their colonies in Asia.

Tobacco – by royal appointment

Tobacco was cultivated intensively in Haiti by the Spanish and was at first prized for its medicinal qualities. It was ground to a fine powder and sniffed to cure headaches and drunk as a decoction to treat ulcers. The consumption of tobacco through smoking was a novelty introduced to the English court of Elizabeth I by Sir Walter Raleigh, who was a keen pipe-smoker.

Nicotiana tabacum

Although the use of tobacco was introduced to the Netherlands by English soldiers, it was the merchants of the East India Company who acclimatized this American plant to Asia and South Africa.

In the 18th century tobacco was regarded as a luxury and was included as a special privilege in the rations given to the officers and seamen of the East India Company.

The famous pipes of Gouda

The vogue for tobacco led to the birth of a new industry – the

manufacture of earthenware pipes. The first factories appeared in the Netherlands around 1610, when the pipe-makers of Gouda were considered to be the best. Each factory put its own mark on the stem of the pipe and 25 different marks have been identified on porcelain pipes made in Gouda.

The taste of tobacco

Although there are a great many varieties of tobacco, with different tastes, smells and burning qualities, it's only after two final processes, "saucing" and "flavoring" that they come into their own. Saucing involves flavoring the leaves with a mixture of glycerine, liquorice and sugar,

lay in the stamping of a design on the highly porous clay before the glaze was fired, which would then be colored by the nicotine.

Smoking or nonsmoking?

Unlike many other Western societies, the Netherlands hasn't yet adopted policies to restrict consumption of tobacco and cigarettes. In restaurants and cafés there are few non-

breathe when first entering some of the coffee-houses. However, tobacco and the smell of smoke are an integral part of the ambience. In the 17th century Dutch painters even created a new genre, paintings of interiors with smokers, of which Adrien Brouwer was the most famous exponent. In these smoky dens customers who hadn't yet collapsed in a state of drunkenness would indulge in all kinds of debauchery. Today's coffee-shops, where tobacco isn't the only weed to be smoked, are simply perpetuating the old tradition of Dutch permissiveness and tolerance.

A city of cigars

Amsterdam is the most impor-tant market in the world for the sale of wrappers, the leaves in which cigars are rolled, which originate in Indonesia. The city is also famous for its cigars, their subtle aroma obtained by mixing between 15 and 20 different kinds of tobacco from Java, Sumatra, Havana, Brazil, etc.

Adriaen Brouwer, Interior of a Tobacco Shop

while in flavoring they're treated with various essences, such as rum or orange.

The mystery pipe

Between 1900 and 1940 a new pipe, known as the mystery pipe or *door-roker*, was all the rage. An image would appear under the glaze as the pipe was smoked. The secret

smoking zones, and as a result you may find it difficult to

SMOKANIA

Meerschaums, ethnic pipes from all over the world, pipes made from wood, earthenware or porcelain, snuffboxes, cigar and opium boxes, hookahs and opium pipes – a paradise for lovers of smoking paraphernalia.
Prinsengracht, 488
☎ 421 17 79
Mon.-Sat. noon-6pm (or by appointment Mon. & Wed.).

Delicious Dutch
cheese

For many people Dutch cheese means either Edam or Gouda. Yet Holland produces many different kinds of cheese and is the top cheese-exporter in the world. It was in the Middle Ages that the Dutch began to specialize in the manufacture of pressed 'uncooked' cheese. Their unique flavor comes from their capacity to age well and the addition of spices from the Moluccas. Dutch cheese can be left to mature and tasted like wine, from the soft, fruity young cheeses to the spicy dryness of the older varieties.

How the cheese is made

Apart from a small amount of goat's cheese *(geitenkaas)*, most cheese in Holland is made from cow's milk. Dutch cows are among the best milk-producers in the world. Each individual animal can produce up to 6,136 liters (1,350 gallons) a year. The milk is made to curdle by adding a fermenting agent and rennet. The whey is then separated from the curd by a process of stirring, and the curd is put into a mould. After it has been

pressed the cheese is immersed in brine for several days. The flavor and texture of the cheese, which ages as it dries, depends on the length of time it's left to mature.

Cheese from the south...

Make sure you taste some of the delicious farm cheeses while you're in Amsterdam. They're famous for their complex flavors, which grow stronger as they age. Gouda comes in

**GLOSSARY FOR
CHEESE-LOVERS**

Kaas: cheese
Boerenkaas:
  farm cheese made
  with unpasteurized
  milk. Look for the
  special seal stamped
  on the crust.
Jong: young
Belegen:
  medium mature
Pittig: full-flavored
Oud: mature
Heel oud: extra mature

wide, flat rounds and can be eaten *jong* (three to six months old), *pittig* (18 months old), *oud* (two years old) or *heel oud* (two and a half years old or more). The older the cheese, the fuller the flavor. Mature Gouda tastes a bit like parmesan. It also comes in a miniature variety, called Amsterdammer, which is always eaten young.

...and the north

Edam is the characteristic little round cheese whose deep yellow crust is covered in a layer of red wax for export. It's drier than Gouda and can also be eaten at different stages: *jong, belegen* (one year old) and *oud* (two years old). Mimolette is another widely exported northern cheese. Its name means "half-soft" and comes from its consistency, which it loses as it ages.

Gouda "nouveau"!

Gouda is made using milk flavored with fresh herbs and, like wine, arrives in the shops at particular times of year. The soft, delicate May Gouda *(meikaas)* is around for only six weeks, from mid-June to the end of July and the Dutch celebrate its arrival, as they

do that of the herring. You can tell *Leidse kaas*, which is flavored with cumin seeds, from Gouda by the famous crossed keys of the city of Leiden

printed on its orange-colored rind. Friesland also produces a cheese flavored with cloves, called *friese nagel kaas*.

Cheese markets

The biggest cheese market in the Netherlands is held in Alkmaar in north Holland on Friday mornings from May to October. Closer to Amsterdam (30km/18.5 miles) is the town of Edam itself, whose very picturesque market is held on Wednesdays in July and August 10am-12.30pm. Here the cheeses are weighed, under the eye of a bowler-hatted inspector.

WHERE TO BUY CHEESE

Here are the addresses where you can find the best mature Dutch farm cheeses, to buy or just taste:
De Kaaskamer van Amsterdam:
Runstraat, 7; ☎ 623 34 83
Mon. noon-6pm, Tue.-Fri. 9am-6pm, Sat. 9am-5pm, Sun. noon-5pm.
Kaashandel Arxhoek Wout:
Damstraat, 17-19; ☎ 622 91 18
Mon.-Fri. 9am-6pm, Sat. 9am-5pm, Sun. 11am-4pm.
Amsterdamse Kaashal:
Lijnbaansgracht, 32
Fri. 9am-6pm,
Sat. 9am-4pm.
If you are in Amsterdam during the week, you can go to the **Albert Cuypstraat Market**, and the **Noordermarkt** on Saturday (see p. 56).

AMSTERDAM
DIAMANTSTAD

INTERNATIONALE DIAMANT TENTOONSTELLING 21 JUNI t/m 14 JULI 1957
Apollohal, dagelijks van 10 - 17 uur en van 19 - 22 uur, toegang f. 1.25

Diamonds
are forever

A jeweler in Antwerp cut the first faceted diamond in 1475. The full splendor of these hard stones can only be appreciated when they're cut in such a way that exploits to the greatest possible extent the laws governing the refraction and reflection of light. The diamond-cutting workshops of Amsterdam were established at the end of the 16th century and have produced some very famous diamonds, such as the Cullinan and the Kohinoor. The unrivaled skill of Amsterdam's diamond-cutters has turned the city into the diamond capital of the world.

The four "c"s

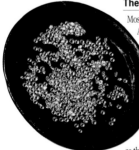

Most of the diamonds cut in Amsterdam originally come from South Africa. They're bought in London, however, at sales called "sights" which take place ten times a year. Diamonds are valued according to four criteria, which are known as the four "c"s. These are the cut, color, clarity and carat – or weight – of the stone.

Pyramid to brilliant

Diamonds are made of carbon crystallized by the combined effects of high pressures and temperatures. In their uncut state they're eight-sided. When cut in half they fall into pyramids, the shape in which they were mounted as jewels in the days before the first rose-cut

THE DIFFERENT CUTS OF DIAMONDS

SQUARE PRINCESS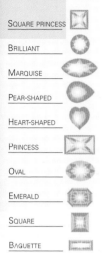

BRILLIANT

MARQUISE

PEAR-SHAPED

HEART-SHAPED

PRINCESS

OVAL

EMERALD

SQUARE

BAGUETTE

was invented. The different types of cut depend on the crystal's initial shape, which may be rectangular, emerald, baguette or oblong, marquise or pear-shaped.

The diamond's sparkle

The most common, but also the most expensive cut is the "brilliant." This consists of a "table" surrounded by 32 upper facets, which slope at an angle of 35° towards the 24 lower facets, themselves sloping at an angle of 41°. A total of 57 facets gives the greatest possible amount of colored sparkle, the "fire" of the diamond.

Subtle colors

A yellowish hue is regarded as highly undesirable in a diamond. However, if, as a result of the presence of another mineral in the carbon at the time of crystallization, a diamond is tinted a uniform pink, blue, green or black, this color gives it an enhanced value.

Purity and brilliance

A high-quality diamond must be completely pure. The over-visible presence of other elements or peculiarities of crystallization (clouds, flaws or feathers) takes away much of its value. Diamonds are classified into seven categories according to a scale of imperfections that are visible to the naked eye (with the aid of a magnifying glass). These range from the Flawless, the purest type, to the kind with the most imperfections, known as Piqué III.

Counting in carats

These precious jewels are weighed in metric carats, one carat being 200 milligrams/ 0.007oz (5 carats = 1gm/ 0.04oz) or a hundred points. A 0.01-carat brilliant has exactly the same number of facets as one weighing 22 carats.

Competitive prices

Besides giving you a greater range of size and quality, buying a diamond in a diamond-cutting shop has the added advantage of being much cheaper than at home. Prices vary from €2,800 to €20,000 per carat, depending on the quality of the stone. So a diamond cut as an emerald costs less than a brilliant for the same

number of carats, since less of the substance is lost. Yellowish coloration and the presence of small inclusions are also factors that make the price of a diamond more affordable.

REAL OR FAKE?

All the diamond-cutters in Amsterdam and all the major jewelers provide certificates of authenticity. These large businesses wouldn't want to undermine their reputations by selling a zircon as a diamond. Better still, they have English speaking sales personnel who are ready to spend the necessary time with you, presenting an entire range of diamonds to suit both your heart and your wallet.

The art of
living in Amsterdam

To make up for the lack of housing in a city that has kept its organic structure almost intact since the 17th century, Amsterdammers have had to be both imaginative and practical. Pioneers of converting old buildings, they invented both lofts and houseboats. Another example of the city's unusual housing is the transformation of its former hospices or *hofjes*.

Loft living

Back in the 1970s, the only place where could you get a reasonably priced room in the center of Amsterdam was on Prinseneiland and Prinsengracht, where the great number of abandoned workshops, disused warehouses and the odd empty church gave architects an enormous choice of spaces to convert as they chose, so long as they preserved the façade. Living without any walls, or conventional layouts, was the challenge for those inventing a non-conformist lifestyle.

Houseboats: life on the water

From old Rhine barges and rafts surmounted by little shacks, to craft that look as

Cozy Corner

It's hardly surprising, in a country where it's wet and windy for most of the year, that Amsterdammers' homes are places of comfort, carefully furnished and decorated and filled with vases of flowers all year round. People here like to be comfortable and their houses tend to be fresh, tidy

though they're going to sink any minute, the floating houses of Amsterdam first appeared on the city's canals in the 1950s, in response to the housing shortage. Originally inhabited by people on the fringes of society, they've become dream homes for the young and those strapped for cash, since a mooring costs only around €450 a year.

Keeping the numbers down

This type of housing was legalized in 1973 as a way of limiting the number of houseboats on the canals, which had a worrying tendency to multiply. Nowadays surveys suggest there's a fleet of 2,400 houseboats, of which only a thousand are licensed, although the others are not actually illegal. They're concentrated on Prinsengracht, Brouwersgracht and the Amstel. Of course, every houseboat is connected to the telephone and the city's supplies of electricity and running water.

Hofjes

Here and there in Jordaan you'll see signs pointing discreetly down narrow alleyways to a *hofje*. These

former hospices, which were originally intended as housing for elderly people in need, consist of tiny houses built round a little courtyard or garden. The *hofjes* have their devotees who, with a few modifications, manage to create little islands of tranquillity for themselves in the bustling heart of the city.

and impeccably clean, with that extra little something that reflects their own special decorative flair. As soon as the sun comes out, the pavements are covered in tables and chairs. This very particular lifestyle is known as *gezelligheid*, which means at once intimate, comfortable and sociable.

SOME THINGS YOU NEED TO KNOW

Pedestrians beware! In Amsterdam the bicycle reigns supreme. Don't even step on to a sidewalk without first checking whether or not it's a cycle track. If it is, a sharp "ding-ding!" will soon remind you of the fact in no uncertain terms. And then there's the question of punctuality. This is a city that runs on time. Don't think you can turn up to meet someone 15 minutes late. Hard work and simplicity are Calvinist virtues; but when the offices close at 5pm, the Dutch like to take some time to relax. After eating their evening meal between 6 and 6.30pm, they like to go on family bike rides, visit their friends or spend the evening in a favorite café.

"Brown cafés"
and *krantcafés*

Cafés have always been a kind of second home to the Dutch, who don't often invite people into their own homes. The decor of the traditional "brown cafés," or *bruine kroegen*, is all nicotine-stained walls, dark wood paneling, sparkling copper pumps and sawdust on the floor. In complete contrast, the interiors of the big cafés are generally light, spacious, and designed with a resolutely contemporary feel. These cafés tend to have a younger clientele.

Krantcafé

The Amsterdammers' favorite pastime is sitting in a café for hours on end reading the newspaper, so it would be unthinkable not to find an enormous range of daily papers *(krant)* on offer in your favorite café. Some large cafés, such as the very cool De Jaren, or the cozier American Café, even provide a large table with good lighting, where you can sit in comfort and read papers all day if you so desire. English-language newspapers are sometimes available too.

The daily grind

After the departure of the office-workers, who come in for their lunch-time snack, the afternoon hours in the cafés are left to the cards and chess players. Aperitif time starts at around 5pm, while

the *eetcafés*, where a portion of the dish of the day *(dagschotel)* tends to be generous and cheap, fill up with young people, who all eat sitting round one big table.

Convivial and cheery

"Brown cafés" tend to be quiet during the day, but liven up in the evening, particularly on Friday and Saturday nights. Regulars and casual customers go there to talk in a free and easy atmosphere without any social pretence. Most drink beer or spirits, some sing songs, others discuss the latest match or set the world to rights with friends who were only strangers an hour ago.

Drinkers' jargon

When you order a beer you'll usually be given a draught lager that is brewed in Amsterdam, either Heineken or Amstel. Try asking for a 20 or 25cl *pils* (about half a pint) or, for the very thirsty, a 50cl *vaas* (about a pint). In both cases the beer should be served with a head two inches thick. The Dutch sometimes drink beer with a little chaser of *jenever* (gin). This strange practice is known as *kopstoot,* or

headbanging, no doubt because of the hangovers it causes.

The *proeflokaal*

Jenever, a spirit distilled from cereals and juniper berries, has its own places of worship, known as *proeflokalen* or tasting-houses. Here, the casks are lined up on the counter and you drink standing up, from a little glass filled to the brim, and you have to suck in the entire contents in one go, without losing a drop. *Jenever* is drunk either young *(jong)* or mellowed with age *(oud)* and is often served with salted herring.

Regular or decaf?

The Dutch love their coffee, so if you're planning to hang out in cafés all day, here are a few things you really ought to bear in mind. One cup of arabica coffee contains between 50

and 100mg of caffeine and the same quantity of robusta coffee contains between 120 and 150mg, while a cup of decaffeinated coffee only contains around 1 or 2mg. Drinking large quantities of coffee (more than nine cups a day) causes a rise in cholesterol levels of between 8 and 10 percent. But a 100mg dose of caffeine stimulates the metabolism, and may increase your expenditure of energy and calories by 16 percent in two hours.

NONSMOKERS, GIVE UP!

The tradition of tobacco smoking has been well-established in Amsterdam since the 17th century and isn't about to fade away. To be sure of this you only have to step inside a "brown café" one evening, when the air is heavy with clouds of smoke. Nonsmokers will almost certainly be happier sitting in one of the larger cafés, which sometimes have designated nonsmoking areas.

Dutch
cuisine

Although the Netherlands is not known for its gourmet cooking or haute cuisine, it does offer a wide selection of tasty meals, and quantities are usually copious. Thanks to the city's varied immigrant communities, delicious spicy food is widely available, including _rijsttafel_, a collection of Indonesian rice dishes.

Flavors of the east

The first Dutch East India Company was founded in Amsterdam in 1594. From their voyages in the Far East, the Dutch brought back a huge quantity of spices, such as pepper, nutmeg, cloves, saffron and chillies, as well as a taste for Indonesian cuisine which has found its way into Dutch cooking.

The _rijsttafel_

The _rijsttafel_ is a dish with a gargantuan selection of Indonesian flavors. It is usually made up of rice, accompanied by around eight (although it can rise to as many as 50) different dishes, including such delicacies as deep fried prawns, chicken kebabs or meatballs with steamed vegetables. This meal is now so much a part of Dutch heritage that the Delft factories have created a specially designed _rijsttafel_ dinner service, with nine different plates that fit together around a central star-shaped dish.

Traditional Dutch cooking

For simple, nourishing Dutch food look out for restaurants displaying the Neerlands Dis sign. Here you can find a hearty meal, including such traditional specialties as split-pea soup flavored with ham, so thick that you can stand a spoon up in it! For a starter try the *bitterballen*, delicious deep fried meatballs from which little clouds of steam escape as you break their crisp breadcrumb crust.

Hutspot

This traditional dish of meat stew with seasonal vegetables commemorates the liberation

How to eat a herring

To eat a *nieuwe haring* the same way as the Dutch, tip your head back, hold your herring by its tail and dangle it into your mouth, then gulp it down in a

dark red patches on their backs. Wash it down with a glass of iced *jenever*.

Seafood, a popular choice

The herring fishing season begins on May 25. The Dutch are great fans of the humble herring and like to eat it raw, seasoned with peppercorns *(nieuwe haring)*. A great many *haringkar* (herring stands) are stationed along the canals all year round, serving *maatsjesharing,* or marinated herrings with onions. Another popular choice for many Dutch people are eels caught in the IJsselmeer *(paling)*, which may be eaten "green" or smoked.

of Leiden, which was besieged by the Spanish in 1574. Legend has it that after the enemy had abandoned their positions, a young boy found a pot of stew which had been left behind and used it to feed the town's starving inhabitants. Although today's ingredients may not be entirely authentic, as the potatoes it invariably contains had not yet found their way on to European tables, it is still recognized as a traditional dish that the people of Leiden consume each year on October 3.

few bites! New herrings should smell of the sea and have no

COFFEE BREAKS

Although the Dutch don't spend much time over their meals, coffee breaks are sacred. *Kopjes koffie* are consumed all day long, usually accompanied by something sweet, such as delicious Droste chocolate pastilles or biscuits flavored with ginger (*speculaas*) or butter. You'll find your will-power crumbling away when faced with a tempting fruit tart or *Limburgse vlaai,* which comes in over 20 different, mouth-watering varieties.

Festivals
in Amsterdam

Sinterklaas (St. Nicholas's Day) and Koninginnedag (Queen's Day) are celebrated throughout the Netherlands, but nowhere more so than in Amsterdam. Unlike most other European countries, the Netherlands celebrates St. Nicholas's Day on December 5 rather than 6, and it's an occasion for family and friends to get together and have fun. On April 30 Amsterdam celebrates Queen's Day with an impressive program of events which attracts over 500,000 people each year.

Patron saint of Amsterdam

St. Nicholas really did exist. Bishop of Myra, he lived from 271 to around 343 AD and was renowned for performing such miracles as calming stormy seas, saving boats from shipwreck, rescuing children from the butcher's knife and putting dowries in the boots of poor young girls. The patron saint of sailors, merchants and children, it was only natural that Amsterdam should be placed under his protection.

Once upon a time…

Today St. Nicholas is the benefactor of all children and the Dutch believe he lives in Spain, where he writes down everything children do in a big red book, while Black Pete, his faithful helper, gets the presents ready for the end of the year. St. Nicholas, dressed in red with a long white beard, rides a white horse, while Black Pete carries a big sack of toys over his shoulder.

A celebration for young and old

Children are generally well behaved at this time of year, as they know St. Nicholas can hear their voices through the chimney. Each night, hoping he will come, they put carrots and hay inside their shoes for his horse. When the great day arrives, Black Pete swaps them

...or a present or a sweet. Adults join in the fun as well and families, friends and colleagues give each other small gifts wrapped in an original style and accompanied by a poem or a riddle. These poems often make fun of the recipient, who has to read them aloud and guess what's inside the package.

Sweet St. Nicholas

Four types of sweets, biscuits and cakes are traditionally eaten around Sinterklaas: *borstplaat* or fondant, *speculaas* or ginger, *letterbanket* and *kerstkrans*. *Borstplaat* is a sort of flat caramel sweet, made with butter or cream, and at this time of year *speculaas*, biscuits are made in the shape of St. Nicholas. *Letterbanket* is made from puff pastry and marzipan and party guests are each given one bearing the first letter of their name. *Kerstkrans* are crown-shaped delicacies covered with glacé fruits, used to decorate the table, and eaten with relish afterwards!

Koninginnedag

Koninginnedag, or Queen's Day, originated on August 31 1898 on Queen Wilhelmina's 18th birthday. When Juliana succeeded her mother she proclaimed that the "Day of the Queen" would be celebrated on

her own birthday, April 30. Her daughter Beatrix, the current reigning monarch, decided to keep the date as 30 April even though her birthday is actually January 31. On Koninginnedag every town in Holland is decked out in orange, the Royal Family's color.

Music and market stalls

On the night of April 29, it's party time in Amsterdam, with singing, dancing and music, and quite a few beers to help things along, of course. Around two million people fill the streets, where actors put on plays, while acrobats amaze

the crowds and Dam Square becomes one big funfair. The following day the big clean-up starts and the city turns into a huge flea market as everyone clears out their junk and sets it out on a stall in the street. On this one day, normal trading licenses are suspended, so anyone can sell whatever they like. You're bound to come home with a bargain you never knew you wanted!

The Vondelpark

On Queen's Day, the Vondelpark is dedicated to children, although parents are encouraged to join in the fun and games. There are races, competitions, games, fishing challenges, and even obstacle courses for bikes with backwards handlebars!

Take to the water!

Many people take out their motor boats, accompanied by friends and a full cargo of beer, naturally, and go to listen to a concert or get together to sing, chat and have some fun. There are so many of these boats that navigation is not always easy and some canals become almost completely blocked, although the atmosphere is always friendly and good-natured.

WHERE TO FIND *SPECULAAS*

Around Sinterklaas the image of St. Nicholas can be found on *speculaas* biscuits in bakeries all over Holland. They come in all shapes and

sizes and look so good it's almost a shame to eat them.

Arnold Cornelis: van Baerlestraat, 93 – ☎ 662 12 28.
Beune: Haarlemmerdijk, 156-158 – ☎ 624 83 56.
Kuyt: Utrechtsestraat, 109 – ☎ 623 48 33.

Practicalities

Getting around

Given that Amsterdam is a comparatively small city where driving is difficult (particularly when it comes to finding a parking place – see p. 6), you're better off exploring the city on foot, taking your bearings from the canals. Apart from Plantage and Pijp, the districts are arranged inside rings of canals encircled by the Singelgracht canal. Allow two days to explore the main attractions, assuming you take a train or boat every now and then to get you from one district to another. If the weather is good, the most pleasant way to get around quickly is still by bicycle, which you can hire for a moderate amount. This is a good way to integrate yourself into the real Amsterdam way of life.

By subway, tram and bus

Services operate from 6am until 12.30am. Night buses take over from 12.30am to 7.30am. The public transport network is extensive, practical, fast and inexpensive: four subway lines, 16 tram lines, four canal-bus links, seven bus lines – including the new "De Opstapper" line which travels the length of Prinsengracht and stops on request – and eight night-bus lines. The majority of trams going from the central station pass along the Dam and Muntplein. For other stops, check the map or ask a driver who will be able to tell you in English. You won't find the subway particularly useful unless you are heading to the east of the city. It is worth noting that if you have hired a bicycle, you can take it on the subway with you. Single tickets (€1.60) can be bought in the subway or from bus and tram drivers. You can save money by buying a travel pass in advance valid for 24 hours (€6.30), 48 hours (€10) or 72 hours (€13). There is also a Strippenkaart, a ticket marked with 15 or 45 boxes (€6.40

see p. 6

AMSTERDAM PASS

This pass is valid for 1, 2 or 3 days (€31, €41 and €51) and offers visitors free use of public transport, a free boat tour of the canals and free admission to 23 museums. It also offers 25 percent reductions at certain restaurants and other attractions. It is great value for museum lovers (admission to museums costs between €4 and €11). The pass is on sale in the VVV tourist offices, the GVB kiosks and in certain hotels.

...and €18.90 respectively) that you have validated by the driver or by a machine (one journey = two boxes). Once your ticket has been validated, you can travel on different forms of transport for a period of one hour, including changes. The cards are on sale in the GVB kiosk opposite the central station, in newspaper shops and from ticket machines in the station, the subway, the Leidseplein or on tram 5. To get on or off the trams or subway trains, press the *deur open* button.

By bicycle

Bicycles have a great many advantages: no parking problems, no hills, absolute priority over cars and pedestrians (who are roundly...

days a week from 9am to 6pm. You will be expected to show an identity card or passport and leave a deposit of €50 to €100 or your credit card details.

Mac Bike
Stationsplein, 12
☎ 620 09 85.
Weteringschans, 2
☎ 528 76 88.
Mr. Visserplein, 2
☎ 620 09 85.
www.macbike.nl
The lowest prices and a huge selection of bicycles for adults and children. If you'll qualify for a group reduction, head for the Mac Bike on Visserplein.

Bike city
Bloemgracht, 68-70
☎ 626 37 21
www.bikecity.nl

This shop offers some good suggestions for routes and provides two locks.

Yellow Bike
Nieuwezijdskolk, 29
☎ 620 69 40
www.yellowbike.nl
The specialist in guided bicycle tours led by an English-speaking guide. (Trips take place Apr.-Oct.: Sun.-Fri. 9.30am and 1pm., Sat. 9.30am and 2pm; advance reservation advisable.)

Frederic Rent a bike
Brouwersgracht, 78
☎ 624 55 09
www.frederic.nl
A reasonable all-inclusive price for classic bicycles.

By pedalo
You can rent a *canal-bike*

abused if they dare put so much as a toe on the sacrosanct cycle lanes), no worries about timetables. The only disadvantage is the possibility of theft, which is quite a common problem. Consequently, when renting a bicycle make sure it comes with a really good lock. The longer the hire period, the cheaper the daily rate. Note that the majority of bicycles have only one gear and a braking system that works by back-pedaling – a little disconcerting at first. Bicycle rental offices are open seven

BY TAXI
There aren't many taxis in the city and they are expensive, so locals tend to use them mostly for journeys at night. You'll find taxi ranks around the central station, on the Dam, Leidseplein, Rembrandtplein, Nieuwmarkt, Waterlooplein and Spui. The central telephone number is ☎ 677 77 77. Although the classic taxi might not be very practical in the city center, you can get to your hotel quickly by water-taxi. Several hotels even have landing stages just for this purpose. Water-taxis are equipped with a standard meter (around €0.90 per minute) and a radio telephone. The most luxurious of them can carry up to eight people (☎ 535 63 63). Bike-taxis (wieler taxi) can carry two people and this is a new and pleasant means of traveling around Amsterdam without getting too footsore! The price of the journey (€1 for 3 mins, €10 for 30 mins) is calculated per person. There is an additional €2.50 reservation fee (☎ 06 28 24 75 50).

(a two- or four-seater pedalo) from the following landing stages: Keizersgracht/ Leidsestraat. The deposit is €50 and the cost is €8 an hour for two people (4 people, €7). A leaflet containing a map of the canals and seven suggested routes is available for €1 and you can return your pedalo to any of the landing stages.

Canal Bike
Weteringschans, 26
☎ 626 55 74
Jun.-end Aug. 10am-9pm,
Sep.-end May 10am-6.30pm.

By boat

Traveling by *canalbus* is fun and particularly pleasant in summer. The three lines provide a shuttle service from the central station to the main points of interests (museums and shopping streets) along the most attractive canals. The red line (five stops towards the east) and the green line (six stops towards the west) run between the station and Rijksmuseum (the whole journey takes 85 mins). The blue line goes to the port, the Nemo and marine museums, the Artis zoo, the Tropenmuseum, the Stopera and Rembrandt's house (journey time of one hour). The *canalbuses* leave every

30 mins (red line), 40 mins (green and blue lines) from 10am to 6pm (until 9pm in July and August).
Canalbus passes cost €1 per person (€11 for children under 13) and cover the whole of the network, allowing you to hop on and off wherever you wish. The tickets are valid until noon on the following day and are sold in the following *canalbus* kiosks: central station, Anne Frank's House, Leidseplein and Rijksmuseum. The pass will give you reductions on the price of entry to museums, other forms of public transport and in certain shops and restaurants. There are candlelit cruises lasting one and a half hours with live jazz music, wine and gouda every Saturday evening from April to November (€42.50). They leave at 8pm and 10pm from in front of the Rijksmuseum (reservation ☎ 623 98 86 or at your hotel).

The museum-boat (*museumboot*) service takes you on a complete tour of the town, starting from the central station and traveling along the most lovely canals. The cruises, with guided commentary, leave every 30 mins (45 mins in winter) from 9.30am to 5pm and make six stops enabling you to visit the museums or do some shopping. You can buy a pass for a whole day (€14.25) or half day (€10.20) from the VVV ticket windows or from the Rederij Lovers kiosk opposite the central station. This will

also give you a 10 to 50 percent off museum entry.

If you like the idea of a one-hour sight-seeing trip on a canal-boat, by day or night, there are a number of organizations offering departures every 15 mins from 9am to 6pm and every 45 mins from 6 to 10pm. You can leave from either the central station or the Rokin.

Last but not least, the best way to tour the canals in real style is to hire an elegant wooden saloon boat, dating from 1920. The captain will see to your every need, you will have access to the bar and you can even order a meal if you so choose. This magnificent saloon boat can cater for a maximum of 12 people. (Salonboot "Paradis," ☎ 684 93 38.)

Telephone and mail

If you are calling the Netherlands from overseas, dial 00 31, followed by the city code without the initial 0 (for Amsterdam 20). To call the US from within the Netherlands, you need to dial 00 1 then the number without the initial 0; the UK is 00 44 then the number without the initial 0. If you're calling an Amsterdam number from within the city itself, you simply need to dial the seven-digit number. If you're calling from elsewhere within the Netherlands, dial 020 before the number. Public telephone boxes are green and marked

MORE INFORMATION

You'll find route maps for all the walks in this chapter at the head of each tour, and references to sights which also appear in the Don't Miss section.

USEFUL ADDRESSES

Police
- General number:
  ☎ 0900 88 44
- Central headquarters, Elandsgracht, 117
  ☎ 559 91 11
- Schiphol: ☎ 603 81 11
- Lijnbaansgracht, 219
- Nieuwezijds Voorburgwal, 104
- Prinsengracht, 1109
- Keizerstraat, 3
- Beurstraat, 33 .

- Open 24 hours:
  – Marnixstraat, 148
  – IJtunnel, 2
  – Linnaeusstraat, 111

Emergency: ☎ 112.

Schiphol Lost Property
☎ 0900 724 47 465.

ATAS (Amsterdam Tourist Assistance Service)
Nieuwezijds Voorburgwal, 104-108
☎ 559 42 51
Every day 10am-10pm.

"PTT telecom." They operate with both coins and the phonecards on sale in post offices, stations, VVV agencies and tobacco shops. Most also accept international credit cards. At the Telecentre (Raadhuistraat, 48), which is open day and night, you can pay using cash, credit card or traveler's check. It is less expensive to call after 6.30pm or at weekends. If you make a call from your hotel room, you will find yourself paying a considerable surcharge. To make your life simpler, you can use one of the many international phonecards that allow you to dial a toll-free number from any telephone booth, and then charge the call to a prepaid account or credit card. Calls from a hotel are subject to surcharges.

You can buy stamps at any post office (open 9am-6pm during the week and until 1pm on Saturdays). You will also find them in shops selling newspapers and postcards. Post letters going outside Holland in the slot marked *overige bestemmingen* on the red PTT mailboxes.

Tourist offices

VVV, Stationsplein, 10; Centraal Station, platform 2; Leidseplein, 12; Schiphol (terminal 2, arrivals hall)
☎ 0 900 400 40 40
(€0.55 per min.)
Mon.-Fri. 9am-5pm
www.visitamsterdam.nl
As well as information leaflets about the city and the surrounding area, you'll find English-speaking staff who can tell you about hotels, forthcoming events and excursions and even make bookings for you if you require. The two big tourist offices in the central station (platform 2: Mon.-Sat. 8am-

8pm, Sun. 9am-5pm; Stationsplein: every day 9am–5pm) are always packed. Alternatively, you will find far fewer people in the tourist office on Leidseplein (every day 9am–5pm), but it's best to find out as much information as possible prior to your trip.

Opening hours

Most museums are open 10am-5pm Monday to Saturday and from 1pm on Sunday. Although the major museums are open every day, some close on Monday and Sunday morning (until 11am or 1pm). On public holidays they follow the Sunday opening hours, with the exception of January 1, 25 December and April 30, when they are closed all day. There are reduced rates for students, children aged 6-18 and senior citizens (over 65) on presentation of a valid ID card.

Banks

Banks are generally open from 9am/10am through 5pm/6pm, Tuesday to Friday, and from 1pm on Monday. They do not close for lunch.

UNEXPECTED AMSTERDAM

Would you like to discover the marvelous gardens hidden behind some of the 17th- and 18th-century mansions and take a look behind the façades of some private houses? André Ancion and his team of art historians and landscape painters organize guided tours on Monday, Friday and Saturday, for small groups of 10 to 20 people (Apr. 15-Sep. 30 and Dec 15.-Feb. 28). Reserve your visit on ☎ 688 12 43 or at www.uhgt.nl. Other themed tours available include the Art Deco and Art Nouveau School of Amsterdam and Contemporary Architecture.

What to see in Amsterdam
and sights not to miss

To help you discover the city, we have planned 14 different walks in Amsterdam, each illustrated by a map. If you only have a limited amount of time, here are 11 sights that you should not miss. They are all referred to within the various suggested itineraries and you will find them described in more detail at the end of the What to See chapter.

Amstelkring Museum

A traditional bourgeois house concealing a clandestine church, used for Catholic worship in the 17th century. An original museum offering something for everyone.

See Walk 5, p. 50 and Don't Miss p. 75

Oude Kerk

A church displaying a variety of architectural styles, whose chimes punctuate the daily life of the locals. It is worth climbing to the top of the bell tower to enjoy the fantastic view of the city.

See Walk 5, p. 50 and Don't Miss p. 72

Nieuwe Kerk

The "new" church actually dates from the 15th century.

Stained glass windows, mahogany pulpit and other treasures. An exceptional backdrop for the ceremonies and recitals that take place there

See Walk 2, p. 42 and Don't Miss p. 73

Amsterdams Historisch Museum

The ideal place to discover everything you need to know about this fascinating city.

See Walk 1, p. 41 and Don't Miss p. 74

Rembrandthuis

Christ Preaching, The Hundred Guilder Print... a huge number of Rembrandt's greater and lesser known works are on display here.

See Walk 6, p. 52 and Don't Miss p. 76

Willet-Holthuysen Museum

Reconstruction of an 18th-century bourgeois house, including kitchen and blue salon. A step back in time.

See Walk 8, p. 59 and Don't Miss p. 78

Het Schip

Signature social housing designed by the architect Michel de Klerk, one of the leading lights of the Amsterdam School of architecture in the early 20th century.

See Culture and Lifestyle p. 12 and Don't Miss p. 79

Van Gogh Museum

Nuenen, Paris, Arles, Auvers-sur-Oise: follow in the footsteps of Van Gogh through the most complete collection of works by this extraordinary painter.

See Walk 11, p. 65 and Don't Miss p. 80

Hortus Botanicus

Herbs and exotic plants in secret gardens right in the heart of the city.

See Walk 12, p. 66 and Don't Miss p. 81

Scheepvaart Museum

Planispheres, astrolabes and even a reproduction three-mast ship. A fascinating collection of all things nautical.

See Walk 12, p. 67 and Don't Miss p. 82

KIT Tropenmuseum

An exotic museum examining many facets of life in tropical countries: reconstructions, a children's museum, store and restaurant.

See Walk 12, p. 67 and Don't Miss p. 83

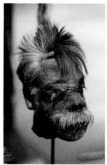

1

Raadhuisstraat

DAM

Soujistraat

Singel

Voorburgwal

Junge Roelensteeg

Wijdest.

7

Singel

St Luciënsteeg

**Amsterdams
Historisch Museum** **4**

Kalverstraat

Rokin

6 **3**

Spuistraat

Nieuwezijds

2 **Begijnhof**

5 **8**

Spui **1**

Singel

Handboogstr.

Voetboogstraat

Kalverstraat

Singel

Heiligeweg

100 m

The Beguinage,
culture and history

A stone's throw from the bustle of Kalverstraat, the Beguinage area is an island of calm centered on Spui square – an elegant triangular space where history and culture meet. You'll find the city's most famous "brown café" here, as well as two trendy cafés, the Beguine convent and a great bookstore.

❶ Spui★★

Once home to the Provos (see p. 14) who used to dance in mad circles round the statue of Livertje, a kind of Amsterdam street urchin symbolizing their rebellious spirit. This square has since been restored and is now the cultural heart of Amsterdam. There is a second-hand book market every Friday and a contemporary art market every Sunday.

❷ Begijnhof★★★

Entrance on the Spui marked by a carved coat of arms
Every day 10am-5pm
Free entry.

A narrow vaulted passageway leads to this charming garden

urrounded by 17th- and
8th-century houses. The
evout Beguine nuns have
een replaced by elderly
adies or female students
f slender means. In the
niddle of the lawn stands
ne medieval church, while
o. 34 is the city's oldest
ouse, built from wood and
ating from 1477.

3 Schuttersgalerij (Gallery of the Civil Guard)

**Mon.-Fri 10am-5pm,
Sat.-Sun. 11am-5pm
Free entry.**

This covered passage, between
he historical museum and the
Beguine convent, houses huge
group portraits of the civil
guards who were once charged
with protecting one of the
eleven districts of the city.
These bourgeois citizens,
dressed as archers, crossbow-
men and soldiers, look as if

they spent more time at the
dining table than on the
battlefield!

4 Amsterdams Historisch Museum★★

**Kalverstraat, 92
Nz Voorburgwal, 357
☎ 523 18 22
www.ahm.nl
Mon.-Fri. 10am-5pm, Sat.
and Sun. 11am-5pm (closed**

Dec. 25, Jan. 1 and Apr. 30)
**Entrance charge
See Don't Miss p. 74.**
The city's history unfolds
step by step in this highly
informative museum housed
in a former orphanage built in
the 15th century and enlarged
in the 17th century. Works of
art, maps and models evoke
the everyday life of the people
of Amsterdam since the 13th
century.

5 Café Hoppe★★

**Spui, 18-20
☎ 420 44 20
Every day 8am-1am
(2am Fri., Sat. and Sun.).**

A real Amsterdam institution,
Café Hoppe has been popular
with both locals and visitors
to the city since 1670. The
narrow, wood-paneled,
smoke-filled room, with
its sawdust-covered floor,
is always packed, even
spilling out into the square
on nice days.

6 Lucius★★

**Spuistraat, 247
☎ 624 18 31
Every day 5pm-midnight.**

This is the best fish restaurant
in town. The dining room is
simply decorated with pottery
and rustic tables and the daily
specials chalked up on the
blackboard. It serves up good,
no-frills fish and seafood
specialties depending on the
day's catch. There is a wide
range of liqueurs to round off
your meal.

8 Atheneum Boekhandel★

**Spui, 14-16
☎ 622 62 48
Mon.-Sat. 9.30am-6pm (9pm
Thu.), Sun. noon-5.30pm.**

Like the square, this lovely
bookstore is very elegant and
extremely busy. Visit the main
shop for the latest best-seller or
CD. Or try the annex next door
for an English newspaper.

7 SQUAT VRANKRIJK★

Although squatting may have gone out of style, a few of
the indomitable old guard bought their squats and turned
the former premises of the *Handelsblad* newspaper into
a kind of living memorial to the huge Provo protest
movement (see p. 14) which flourished in the 1970s. The
brightly colored tags and graffiti, the "kill the police" sign
pasted on the façade and the grunge evenings are just a
pale reflection of how things used to be.

Spuistraat, 199-216.

2

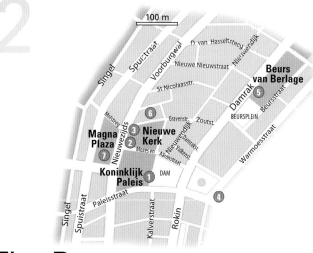

The Dam,
Amsterdam's true heart

This is the beating heart of the city, where there's always something going on amid the neon signs and fast-food outlets. Around the square, monuments testify to the Calvinist philosophy of money, religion and hard work, values attacked by the Provos, who made their headquarters here. The stark concrete obelisk commemorating Dutch victims of war has become a meeting point for new-style hippies, punks and dropouts.

❶ Koninklijk Paleis★

☎ 620 40 60
www.koninklijkhuis.nl
Mon., Thu., Fri. and Sat.
12.30-5pm; Jul. and Aug.
every day 11am-5pm
Entrance charge.

Before becoming the royal residence of Louis Bonaparte, this inelegant, austere building was the town hall, designed by the famous 17th-century architect Jacob van Campen. Don't miss the superb tiled floor in the Burghers' Hall (Burgerzaal) decorated with maps of the northern and southern hemispheres. Today the queen comes here only for official receptions.

❷ Nieuwe Kerk★★

☎ 626 81 68
www.nieuwekerk.nl
Open every day during
temporary exhibitions
10am-6pm (10pm Thu.)
Entrance charge
See Don't Miss p. 73.

The New Church was built in the flamboyant gothic style and has been modified many

times over the years. Today it plays host to exhibitions and concerts. Its stained glass, bronze chandeliers, mahogany pulpit (1649) and superb choir stalls are perfectly complemented by the sparse, Calvinist interior. In accordance with tradition, all the Dutch kings and queens have been crowned here.

❸ Palette★

Nz Voorburgwal, 125
☎ 639 32 07
Sat. 11am-5pm and by appointment in the week.

Leaning up against the Nieuwe Kerk is the city's smallest shop, specializing in making silk and satin shoes. With a choice of over 500 colors, there is no way you could fail to find just the right shoes and accessories to go with your favorite evening dress.

❹ Hotel Krasnapolsky★

Dam, 9
☎ 554 91 11
Open 24 hours.

Whether you want a cup of tea or dinner, this 20th-century, 5-star palace should be your first stop. It boasts a vast and astounding winter garden, which recalls the past splendor of the Belle Époque.

❻ DE DRIE FLESCHJES★★

The city's finest *proeflokaal* was first founded by the Bootz distillery in 1650. This is the place where journalists and stockbrokers congregate at the end of the day, hanging their jackets on the taps of the barrels before drinking a few *borrels* of gin. They also have a unique collection of portraits of the mayors of Amsterdam here, all painted on little bottles.

Gravenstraat, 18 – ☎ 624 84 43 – Every day 2-10.30pm.

The decor in the restaurant features of black and white floor tiles, frescoes on the walls and tall palm-trees. To cap it all, the food is excellent too (buffet-style lunch and breakfasts).

❺ Beurs van Berlage★★★

Beursplein, 1
☎ 530 41 41
www.beursvanberlage.nl
For visits (groups of ten or more people, entrance charge) contact Artifex Travel (☎ 620 81 12).

This imposing building sited along the Damrak, has a red-brick façade 141m (463ft) long, designed by H. P. Berlage. In 1903 its sober, functional style represented an astonishing break with the past. It is the home of the Dutch Philharmonic Orchestra and the grand hall has ideal

acoustics for concerts. During restoration work on the building (guided tours only) you can catch a glimpse of the B Van B café (Tue.-Sun. 10am-6pm), on the ground floor, which organizes a big theme night on the first Friday of every month

❼ Magna Plaza★

Nz Voorburgwal, 182
☎ 626 91 99
Mon. 11am-7pm, Tue.-Wed. and Fri.-Sat. 10am-7pm (9pm Thu.), Sun. noon-7pm.

This pretentious neo-gothic construction in brick and white stone earned its architect, Cornelis Peters, more than a few sarcastic comments in 1899. Originally the central post office, it has since been transformed into an elegant shopping center. The stairwell is definitely worth seeing.

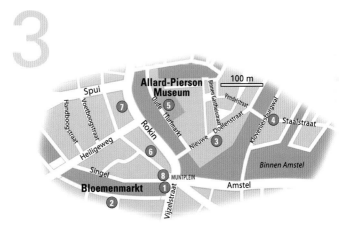

The Rokin,
for a Saturday stroll

Once a favorite haunt of Amsterdam's bourgeoisie, who would promenade along the side of the inner dock (*rak-in*), this was home to the most prestigious establishments in the city. The large banks, the best diamond merchants, the most prominent antique dealers and Hajenius, cigar-makers since 1826, could all boast that their clientele included royalty. Today, the dock has been filled in to make way for cars and trams, and the upscale businesses find themselves sharing their space with other, less exclusive shops.

❶ Munttoren★

Muntplein, 12.

In 1620, Hendrick of Keyser used the remains of an old city gate as a base on which to build a baroque wooden bell tower, housing a chiming clock that still rings out every quarter of an hour. The tiny shop on the ground floor sells genuine Delft and Makkum ware.

❷ Bloemenmarkt ★★

**Singel / Muntplein
Mon.-Sat. 8am-5.30pm and
Sun. 9am-5pm in summer.**

The flower-sellers' barges are permanently moored on the Singel, forming a brightly colored floating market. The stalls displaying cut and

dried flower stalls, valuable bonsais and heaps of bulbs make for an unforgettable spectacle.

❸ Café De Jaren★

Nieuwe Doelenstraat, 20-22
☎ 625 57 71
Every day 10am-1am
(2am Fri. and Sat.).

This is the most fashionable of the large cafés, designed by Onno de Vries, and an attractive, light space located along the Amstel. In fine weather, you may have to fight for a table on the huge floating terrace. Popular with everyone from students to businesspeople, and an excellent spot for a late breakfast or quick lunch.

❹ Staalstraat★★

This charming street straddles two canals by means of drawbridges. It is lined with numerous shops, including the art bookshop Nijhot & Lee and the Puccini confectioner's shop. The attractive gabled house at no. 7B is the former drapers' hall, headquarters of the guild of drapers whose portraits were painted by Rembrandt (*Drapers' Guild* at the Rijksmuseum, see p. 64).

❽ ANDRIES DE JONG SHIP SHOP★

If you've always dreamt of turning your home into a pleasure-cruiser, look no further. This shop sells barometers, storm lamps, cabin lamps, pirate flags, compasses and every conceivable gadget for people with a passion for ships and sailing.

Muntplein, 8 – ☎ 624 52 51
Mon.-Fri. 9am-5.30pm, Sat. 10am-6pm.

❺ Allard-Pierson Museum★★

Oude Turfmarkt, 127
☎ 525 25 56
Tue.-Fri. 10am-5pm,
Sat., Sun. and holidays
1-5pm
Entrance charge.

A tiny but very informative archeological museum where you can learn about the everyday lives of the mediterranean peoples of Antiquity through objects and models. You can also see your name written in hieroglyphics on the computer and admire the superb Parthian and Sassanid jewelry.

❻ La Maison de Bonneterie★

Rokin, 140
☎ 531 34 00
Mon. 1-5.30pm,
Tue.-Sat. 10am-5.30pm
(9pm Thu.), Sun. noon-5pm.

This is a real, old-fashioned department store, boasting the title "Supplier to the Queen." It has three floors where you can still buy timeless, quality products such as classic, hard-wearing British clothing for the whole family, or a set of golf clubs and accessories. The brasserie on the first floor is just as quaint, filled with respectable old ladies taking their afternoon tea.

❼ P.G.C. Hajenius★★

Rokin, 92-96
☎ 623 74 94
Tue.-Sat. 9.30am-6pm (9pm Thu.), Sun.-Mon. noon-6pm.

This place really is an Amsterdam institution. The prestigious Hajenius cigar-maker's, with its cozy decor of cedar-wood, marble, lamps and accessories in pure art-deco style, has been making subtly blended aromatic cigars for 175 years.

4

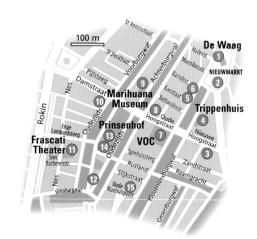

From Nieuwmarkt
to Prinsenhof

The shady canals are lined with traditional shops and former convents, now converted into cafés, giving this picturesque university quarter its special character. Here you'll find experimental theaters and secondhand book-stalls, cannabis-smokers and herring-eaters. This is village Amsterdam, where everybody knows everybody else.

❶ De Waag★
Nieuwmarkt, 4
☎ **422 77 72**
Every day 10am-midnight.

In the 17th century the massive turreted St. Anthony Gate, a rare remnant of the medieval fortified wall, was used as the public weighing station (*waag*). The hall on the upper floor, previously occupied by the Surgeons' Guild, was where Rembrandt painted his first famous picture: *The Anatomy*

Lesson of Professor Tulp. Decorated by Jaap Dÿkmann, today the hall is a friendly café and restaurant entirely lit by candles, giving it a particularly magical atmosphere after dark. A fashionable place to grab a quick lunch, sample the tapas (from 5pm) or enjoy a simple dinner with friends (until 10.30pm), De Waag has one of the most attractive open-air eating areas in the city.

❸ Biba★★

Nieuwe Hoogstraat, 26
☎ 330 57 21
Mon. 1-6pm, Tue.-Sat.
11am-6pm, Sun. 1-5pm.

You might find it difficult to leave this small shop empty-handed, with its fairy-tale jewelry by names such as Otazu, Jean-Paul Gaultier, Vivienne Westwood, John Hardy and Erikson Beamon. You will also find a range of very chic rings for €40 as well as a necklace design worn by Hillary Clinton (€1,699) and bags decorated with pearls and fake gemstones. If you are after some Dutch designs, the Gem Kingdom range offers a fine marriage of silver and turquoise.

❹ Trippenhuis★★

Kloveniersburgwal, 29.

This imposing old building, built in the Renaissance style in 1660, is one of the few in Amsterdam that can compete with the grandeur of the Venetian palaces. Its owners, the Trip brothers, had made their fortunes from the arms business. Across the canal, at no. 26, you can see the much more modest establishment which was once the home of their coachman.

❺ Herboristerie Jacob Hooy & Cie★

Kloveniersburgwal, 12

☎ 624 30 41
Mon.-Fri. 10am-6pm,
Sat. 10am-5pm.

For 150 years members of the Oldenboom family have stood behind the counter of this deliciously spicy-smelling shop. The wooden casks that line the shelves and the polished drawers contain around six hundred different aromatic plants. The delicious liquorice sweets are not to be missed.

❻ De Bekeerde Suster★★

Kloveniersburgwal, 6-8
☎ 423 01 12
Every day noon-1am
(2am Fri. and Sat.).

This new café-brasserie is inside the former Bethany convent, which used to provide a home for "lost women" – from where it got its name, "converted sister." It specializes in bitter artisan beers (Wit Ros) or seasonal beers (Bockros), brewed in the huge copper vats in the backroom. Food takes the form

of daily specials and there is also a variety of types of gin available.

❼ VOC Building

Oude Hoogstraat, 24.

In the 17th and 18th century, this large building of red brick and yellow stone, bearing the monogram of the Vereenige Oostindische Compagnie, was the headquarters of the famous Dutch East India Company, which imported spices, colored fabrics and porcelain from the East. Public sales of these goods were held twice a year in the courtyard.

❷ NIEUWMARKT SQUARE

The city council called on two Dutch sculptors, Alexander Schabracq and Tom Postma, to revamp Nieuwmarkt. These two artisans, who also worked on the Damrak, are responsible for the green railings and lamp-posts inspired by the Russian constructivist movement. Not everybody likes these new additions, but at least they don't get in anyone's way.

in the manufacture of hemp ropes.

❿ Manus Magnus★★

Oudezijds Voorburgwal, 268
☎ 622 68 12
Tue.-Fri. 10am-6pm, open the first and last weekend of the month.

Manus Magnus works with gold and silver to create stunning items such as dishes and candlesticks, with mirror-smooth or brushed surfaces across which the light dances. When he mixes the two metals his creations have an organic feel, as though uprooted directly from the earth. If you have a particular idea in mind you can commission him to realize the design for you.

❽ Capsicum★★

Oude Hoogstraat, 1
☎ 623 10 16
Mon. 11am-6pm, Tue.-Sat. 10am-6pm.

The artist's palette of colors and shimmering materials, with classical music in the background seduce the customer in this upscale store selling fabric for furnishings and dress-making. The majority of the linens, cottons and silks come from India and Thailand, including some wonderful silk brocade (their specialty), as well as swaths of muslin and tie-dyed cotton. Expect to pay between €20 and €60 per meter (yard) for plain cotton.

❾ Marihuana Museum★

Oudezijds Achterburgwal, 148
☎ 623 59 61
Every day 11am-11pm Entrance charge.

If you want to know more about marijuana and its various uses, this museum – the only one of its kind in Europe – is the place for you to visit. It retraces the 10,000-year history of cannabis. You will discover that before being grown in people's cellars and sold in the coffee-shops, it was used extensively in the port of Amsterdam... but only

⓫ Frascati Theater★

Nes, 63
☎ 626 68 66
www.nestheathers.nl
Performances: 8.30 or 9pm

This small, experimental theater specializes in contemporary plays and choreography. You do not always need to understand Dutch to watch one of these sometimes disconcerting shows. The café next door, De Blinker, serves light meals until 9.30pm and attracts a crowd of theater-goers.

children holding out their hands for food at each stop. This was the subject he chose to paint in 1949 and it was accepted by the town hall in lieu of the tax he owed.

⓰ Oude Manhuispoort Passage★

Book fair:
Every day 10am-6pm.
The secondhand booksellers set up their stalls in the alcoves of the covered passageway linking the two canals, Oudezijds Achterburgwal and the Kloveniersburgwal, right in the heart of the university district. Take a look

at the lovely inner courtyard and flick through the old engravings that will give you a sense of the Amsterdam of years gone by.

⓬ House of the Three Canals★★

Intersection of Oudezijds Voorburgwal, Oudezijds Achterburgwal and Grimburgwal canals.

This fine old building from the Golden Age of the 17th century, with its distinctive red shutters and two-tone façade, was built at the point where three canals meet and was the last building to the southeast of the medieval city of Amsterdam. Today it houses a publishing company.

⓮ Café Roux★

Oudezijds Voorburgwal, 197
☎ 555 35 60
Open every day noon-2.30pm and 6-10.30pm.
This art-deco brasserie is one of the best recommendations in Amsterdam if you like French regional cuisine or just a good cup of tea. A fresco by Karel Appel adorns the walls – the artist was traveling by train through war-ravaged Europe and was haunted by the large-eyed

⓭ Prinsenhof★★★ (The Grand Hotel)

Oudezijds Voorburgwal, 197
☎ 555 35 60.
In the 16th century this luxury hotel was the residence of princes. It is still called the "Court of Princes" despite the fact that until 1986 it was the town hall (after the town hall along the Dam was transformed into the royal palace). In 1966, the marriage of Queen Beatrix was held in the art-deco wedding hall.

House of the Three Canals

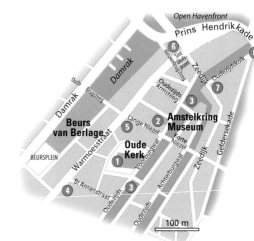

The red-light district,
where anything goes

This is one of the most visited districts of Amsterdam, and you can hardly blame tourists for sneaking a peep at the scantily clad women who wait for customers in their windows. The district is relatively quiet during the day, but livens up at night when the red neon signs are lit. Inquisitive visitors throng the quayside, while delicious smells of Chinese cooking waft down from Zeedijk, home to Amsterdam's unassuming Chinatown. The biggest irony is the contrast of the sacred and profane provided by the district's two churches, one of which is hidden away in an attic.

❶ Oude Kerk★★ (Old Church)

Oude Kerksplein, 23
☎ 625 82 84
www.oudekerk.nl
Mon.-Sat. 11am-5pm,
Sun. 1-5pm
Entrance charge
Bell-ringing concert
Sat. 4–5pm
See Don't Miss p. 72.

With the tiny houses clinging to its sides, the Old Church looks like a ship cast adrift in the middle of an ocean of sin. Both its octagonal, gothic/

Renaissance style bell tower and the rest of the building was once a landmark for sailors. It did not escape the iconoclastic fury of the Calvinists in the late 16th century, which explains the sparseness of its interior. It is sometimes used for concerts.

❷ Amstelkring Museum★★★

Oudezijds Voorburgwal, 40
☎ 624 66 04
www.museumamstelkring.nl

Mon.-Sat. 10am-5pm,
Sun. 1-5pm (closed Jan. 1
and Apr. 30)
Entrance charge
See Don't Miss p. 75.

Hidden in the attic of this sweet little bourgeois house is a clandestine chapel that was established in 1663 after Catholics lost their right to worship. The house, with its heavy Dutch furniture, table-coverings, two kitchens decorated with Delft tiles and numerous interesting nooks and crannies, is worth a visit.

❸ Oudezijds Voorburgwal★

It was almost inevitable that this canal, a stone's throw from the old port, would become the headquarters of the city's red-light district. In red neon-lit windows, barely dressed women make phone calls, dance, read magazines or simply gaze out at what is going on in the street to pass the time between clients. Here there can be no mistaking what trade is being plied.

❹ Condomerie Het Gulden Vlies

Warmoes-
straat, 141
☎ 627 41 74
Mon.-Sat.
11am-6pm.

The threat of AIDS has boosted the sale of condoms, which now come in an amazing range of colors and tastes, and some very improbable shapes, such as cow's udders, hands, Mickey Mouse figures and dummies. Plenty of amusing gift ideas.

❺ Geels & Co★★

Warmoesstraat, 67
☎ 624 06 83
Mon.-Sat. 9.30am-6pm.

This shop has been selling excellent coffee, ground on the premises, for the last 150 years. The owners will be only too pleased to show you their collection of roasting machines and mills on display upstairs.

❻ In de Olofspoort★★★

Nieuwebrugsteeg, 13
☎ 624 39 18
Tue.-Thu. 4pm-midnight,
Fri.-Sat. 4pm-1am.

One of Amsterdam's best *proeflokaals* is hidden behind the attractive Renaissance façade designed by Hendrick de Keyser in 1619. This café is not linked to a particular gin producer and offers a huge range of *jenevers* and liqueurs such as "my aunt's water" and one flavored with *speculaas*. These should be enjoyed in the appropriate glass, accompanied by spicy anecdotes and advice from the owner.

❼ Cirelli restaurant★★

Oudezijds Kolk, 69

☎ 624 35 12
Every day from 6pm,
closed Sun. in winter
Reservation advisable.

This former warehouse, renovated with a touch of imagination, serves the best pasta in town. Look out for the sculpture by Alexander Schabracq on the central table and the wonderful lamps.

❽ Schreierstoren★ (The Tower of Weeping Women)

Prins Hendrikkade, 94-95
☎ 624 80 52
Café (☎ 428 82 91):
Mon. 10am-7pm, Tue.-Thu.
10am-1am, Sat. 10am-3am,
Sun. 11am-8pm
Shop (☎ 624 80 52):
Mon.-Sat. 10am-6pm.

It's said that sailors' wives would stand at the top of this tower watching their loved ones sail into the distance, possibly never to return. It now houses a coffee-shop on the first floor and on the second a shop selling almanacs, sky charts and the very expensive Bolle barometers.

> ## QUOTATION
>
> *"Like opulent ladies by Rubens, they sit in their armchairs, next to a vase of paper roses, in the intimate lamp light. In Amsterdam, even vice assumes an old-fashioned air of warm and meditative bonhomie."* Klaus Mann, 1952.

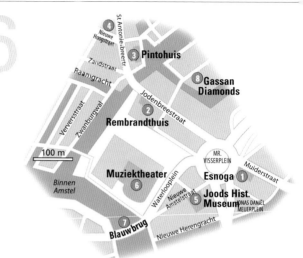

6

St Antoniebreett
Nieuwe Hoogstraat
❹
❸ Pintohuis
Zandstraat
Raamgracht
❽ Gassan Diamonds
Jodenbreestraat
Verversstraat
Zwanburgwal
❷
Rembrandthuis
100 m
MR. VISSERPLEIN
Muiderstraat
Binnen Amstel
Muziektheater ❻
Waterlooplein
Nieuwe Amstelstraat
Esnoga ❶
❺ Joods Hist. Museum
JONAS DANIËL MEIJERPLEIN
❼
Blauwbrug
Nieuwe Herengracht

The old Jewish quarter,
after renovation

Cross the Amstel and you enter a ghost town dominated by the highly controversial Stopera complex. The building of the metro and the drive towards better housing have all but finished the destruction that began in World War Two, though Jewish people still gather here on Saturdays in the large synagogue. Other surviving interest includes the Rembrandt House, the Jewish Historical Museum and Gassan Diamonds.

❶ Esnoga★★★ (Portuguese Synagogue)

Mr. Visserplein, 3
☎ 624 53 51
Apr. 1-Oct. 31: Sun.-Fri.
10am-4pm; Nov. 1-Mar. 31:
Sun.-Thu. 10am-4pm,
Fri. 10am-3pm
Entrance charge.

This enormous brick cube with its huge windows really is a synagogue, and one of the most beautiful in Europe. Financed by the community of Portuguese Jews, descended from those driven from their country by the Spanish Inquisition, it miraculously

still looks just the way it did when it was first opened back in 1675.

❷ Rembrandthuis★★

Jodenbreestraat, 4-6
☎ 520 04 00
www.rembrandthuis.nl
Mon.-Sat. 10am-5pm,
Sun. 1-5pm (closed Jan. 1)
Entrance charge
See Don't Miss p. 76.

Rembrandt bought this superb Renaissance house in 1639 with his wife Saskia's dowry. He lived here for 20 years, painting his finest pictures in his first-floor studio. But a different aspect of the artist's

formidable talent is on show here in a display of 250 engravings arranged by

theme, including genre scenes, self-portraits, nudes and landscapes.

❸ Pintohuis★

Sint Antoniesbreestraat, 69
☎ 624 31 84
Mon. and Wed. 2-8pm,
Fri. 2-5pm, Sat. 11am-4pm
Free entry.

In 1651 Isaac Pinto, a rich Jewish banker, spent a tidy sum buying himself this lovely Italianate palace, which certainly stands out in this much altered district. In the 1970s it narrowly escaped the bulldozers and was turned into a library. Some of the original paintings remain on the ceiling of the ground floor, along with some gilded garlands on the beams of the room on the first floor.

❹ Joe's Vliegerwinkel★

Nieuwe Hoogstraat, 19
☎ 625 01 39
Mon. 1-6pm, Tue.-Fri.
11am-6pm, Sat. 11am-5pm.

A real delight for children of all ages, this shop, packed full of kites in all shapes and sizes, is definitely worth a detour. Made on the premises or imported from China and the USA, the kites are constructed

from multicolored nylon, and have all been selected for their sheer beauty and originality.

❺ Joods Historisch Museum★

Jonas Daniël Meijerplein, 2-4
☎ 626 99 45
www.jhm.nl
Every day 11am-5pm

Entrance charge.
This museum is housed in four synagogues of the Ashkenazi community,

connected by glass walls and walkways. Objects, photographs and documents are arranged thematically to illustrate the life and culture of the Jews who have lived in Amsterdam since the late 16th century.

❻ Muziektheater "Stopera"★★

Waterlooplein, 22/Amstel, 3
☎ 551 89 11
Guided tours: ☎ 551 80 54.

The enormous complex that towers over the Amstel houses the new town hall and a concert hall with seats for 1,600 people. The building's highly controversial aesthetics, and the extra destruction it necessitated in a district that had already been blighted by town planners, generated some violent reactions. It opened in 1986 and is still known as "Stopera," the name given to it by its critics ("Stop-the-opera"). It does, however, have remarkable acoustics.

❼ Blauwbrug★ (Blue Bridge)

Built for the universal exhibition of 1883, this bridge crosses the majestic Amstel. It was this river on which the city was first founded, and which also gave it its name: "Amstel-dam."

❽ GASSAN DIAMONDS★★★

Nieuwe Uilenburgerstraat, 173-175
☎ 622 53 33
Every day 9am-5pm, free tour every 20 mins.

Gassan is the biggest diamond house in Holland. An expert guide will talk you through the work of the stone polishers, and explain all about facets, what makes a diamond valuable and, above all, the traps to avoid when making a purchase.

The best time to take a tour is first thing in the morning or between 1pm and 3pm, when it's quieter.

7

Jordaan,
popular Amsterdam

This is the district that Amsterdammers like best. With its tight network of narrow streets and houses, its nicotine-stained "brown cafés," little courtyards full of flowers, tiny shops, barge-filled canals and colorful bird market, it's here that the very soul of the city lies. The district was built outside the city walls in the 17th century to house working-class laborers, with Prinsengracht forming a natural border with the world of the middle classes. Although somewhat gentrified these days, it retains its own language and folklore, which come to the fore during the Jordaan festival in September.

❶ Westerkerk★★ (Western Church)

Westerplein
Clock tower visit Apr.-Sep.:
Mon.-Sat. 10am-4pm
Bell-ringing concert Sun. noon-1pm
Entrance charge.

Regarded as Hendrick de Keyser's masterpiece, this was the first Renaissance-style church to be built after the Reformation. At the top of the 85m (280ft) bell tower you can see the Imperial crown, added to

the city's coat of arms by Emperor Maximilian of Austria.

❷ Coppenhagen, 1001 kralen★

Rozengracht, 54
☎ 624 36 81
Mon. 1-6pm, Tue.-Fri. 10am-6pm, Sat. 10am-5pm.

On the shelves of this shop you'll see hundreds of jars filled with gleaming glass beads of every conceivable color, including antique beads from

Murano and Bohemia, which were once used to trade with African princes, and more recently made beads from India, Indonesia, Germany and Venice.

❸ Anne Frankhuis★

Prinsengracht, 267
☎ 556 71 00
www.annefrank.nl
Every day 9am-7pm
(9pm Apr.-end Aug.;
closed Yom Kippur)
Entrance charge.

If you're not deterred by the long lines, you can visit the *achterhuis*, or "house behind," where the adolescent Anne Frank lived hidden away with the rest of her family, eight people in all, for two years before being deported and dying in Bergen-Belsen concentration camp. Her personal diary, which gives a poignant account of this time, has been published in almost 50 different languages. The money raised from sales of the book is partly used to fund the Anne Frank Foundation, which fights against racism.

❹ Bloemgracht★

In the 17th century, the "canal of flowers" was inhabited by cloth-dyers. Today it is one of the smartest canals in Jordaan, lined with beautiful gabled houses bearing coats of arms identifying the trades of the original occupants. Three of these, nos. 87, 89 and 91, have been restored to their original, 17th-century glory.

❺ Sint Andrieshofje★★

Egelantiersgracht, 107
Free entry.

Step through the door beneath the coat of arms and, at the end of a passage with a Delft-tiled floor, you'll be surprised to find a small flower-filled garden

Anne Frankhuis

(*hof*) surrounded by tiny houses, once occupied by elderly people in need. The former Beguine convent, founded in 1616, is today one of the most sought-after places to live in the city and a house here is cripplingly expensive.

❻ 't Smalle★★

Egelantiersgracht, 12
☎ 623 96 17
Mon.-Fri. 10am-1am,
Sat. and Sun. 10am-2am.

This café has been a popular venue in the Jordaan district

since 1780, so the nicotine has had more than enough time to impregnate its walls and furniture. Note the pretty enameled stained glass windows and polished tables and chairs. Queen Beatrix herself came here to sample the cozy atmosphere but she stayed outside on the floating terrace, which becomes packed at the first hint of sunny weather.

❼ Greenpeace★

On the corner of Keizers-gracht and Leliegracht.

The campaigning environmental organization Greenpeace is housed in this attractive art-nouveau building built by Gerrit van Arktl in 1905. The imposing façade is enlivened with mosaics, bow windows and pinnacles. Take a look at the ceramics in the entrance hall.

Greenpeace building (p. 55)

❽ Mecanisch Speelgoed★

Westerstraat, 67
☎ 638 16 80
Mon.-Fri. 10am-6pm, Sat.
10am-5pm, closed Wed.
and Sun.

This little shop sells reproductions of lovely old-
fashioned toys, the sort that
you may have seen at your
grandparents' house. The two
floors are packed with masks,
games of patience and skill,
and a variety of painted-metal
clockwork toys.

❾ Claes Claesz in de Jordaan

Egelantiersstraat, 24-26
☎ 625 53 06
Wed.-Sun. 6-11pm.

Step through the wooden door
and you'll find yourself in one
of Jordaan's secret places, a
former hospice founded by a
rich draper in 1616. Today it is
a favorite haunt of students at
the conservatory of music. The
little adjoining restaurant
serves generous portions of

no-frills food, accompanied by
live music at weekends.

❿ Noordermarkt★

On Saturday mornings there's
a bird market on this very
picturesque square, with
homing pigeons, exotic birds
and cages full of cheeping
chicks ranged alongside the
stalls selling fresh farm produce.

⓫ Brouwersgracht★★

The Brewers' Canal marks the
northernmost edge of this
district. With its many bridges,
red-shuttered warehouses
converted into lofts and flower-
decked houseboats moored
along the quaysides, this is one
of the most picturesque views
in the city.

⑫ Aarde-Shirdak★

Westerstraat, 10
☎ 423 32 10
Mon. and Wed.-Sat.
10am-5pm.

This emporium contains piles of the treasures collected by Marianne and Annemieke in the course of their frequent trips to Afghanistan, Pakistan, Central Asia and India. Tempting acquisitions might include old doors and pediments from houses in Nuristan, carved Rajput wardrobes, Kirghiz children's slippers, ethnic clothes and jewelry and heavy stone plates, as well as felt hats and slippers, contemporary creations by the Russian Alexander Pilin.

⑬ 't Papeneiland★★

Prinsengracht, 2
☎ 624 19 89
Mon.-Thu. 10am-1am,
Fri. and Sat. 10am-2am,
Sun. noon-1am.

Gleaming beer pumps, an old cast-iron stove in the middle of the room and walls lined with Delft tiles constitute the decor of this small "brown café" that has been popular with the locals since 1642.

⑭ Koevoet★

Lindenstraat, 17
☎ 624 08 46
Dinner from 6pm, except
Sun. and Mon.

An unpretentious little *eetcafé* of the kind that flourishes in Jordaan. You enter via an old bar with a well-worn floor, then, up some steps, you reach the small dining room itself, where you'll find a few buffet tables set out in a welcoming manner.

⑯ Noorderkerk (Northern Church)

The Northern Church is the Western Church's little sister and was designed by the same architect, Hendrick de Keyser. It was especially built for the Protestant inhabitants of Jordaan, who found the Westerkerk too grand for their comfort. This is one of the few churches where services are still held.

⑮ THE VAN WEES DISTILLERY★

Driehoeckstraat, at the very end of Brouwersgracht, is home to the oldest distillery in the Netherlands, owned by the Van Wees family, who have passed down from generation to generation the secret of making *jenever* flavored with herbs. If you want to sample the products, however, you need to press on to the De Admiraal *proeflokaal* at no. 319 Herengracht (see p.132).

8

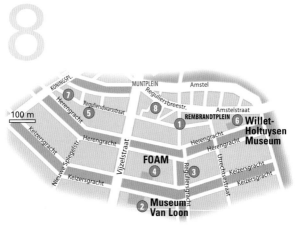

Rembrandtplein,
grand houses and gay club

By day this district between the Amstel and Keizersgracht is a place of quiet squares and shady canals whose still waters mirror the magnificent facades of palatial residences, some of which reveal their secrets to visitors. But once the strings of lights between the seven bridges of Reguliersgracht are switched on, the night revelers invade the streets and the area reveals its livelier side, full of fast-food outlets and gay bars.

❶ Rembrandtplein★

Former home to the old butter market, this square was renamed after the great 17th-century master painter, whose statue stands in its center. Today it's full of cafés, of varying degrees of stylishness, with tables and chairs spilling out over the sidewalk, and is one of the main hangouts for young Amsterdammers.

❷ Museum Van Loon★★★

Keizersgracht, 672
☎ 624 52 55
www.museumvanloon.nl
Fri.-Mon. 11am-5pm (Jul.-Aug. every day 11am-5pm)
Entrance charge.

The heir to the Van Loon fortune has opened the doors of his family residence, and invites you into the cosseted world of the 18th-century patrician. With its silk wall hangings, chests made from exotic wood, family portraits and tables displaying valuable porcelain, this is one of the city's most delightful places.

This ultra-contemporary venue acts as a new platform for the visual arts with exhibitions throughout the year, changing every three months, of photographs and videos by the great international photographers. Hanging on the ground floor are works by younger and as yet unknown photographers.

❸ Hooghoudt★★

Reguliersgracht, 11
☎ 420 40 41
Mon. 4-8pm,
Tue.-Sat. 4pm-midnight.

Once the working day is over, this *proeflokaal*, housed in an old 17th-century warehouse, is standing room only. Here they drink Groningen *jenever*, which is kept in earthenware jars to preserve its special flavor. Start by ordering an iced *korenwijn* (wheat wine). Then you can sit down to enjoy Dutch delicacies such as eel braised in butter.

❹ FOAM★★ (Museum of Photography)

Keizersgracht, 609
☎ 551 65 00
www.foam.nl
Every day 10am-5pm (9pm Thu.-Fri.); closed Jan. 1
Entrance charge.

Three 18th-century aristocratic homes and their gardens have been linked by a cunning system of passageways designed by the architect Benthem Crouwel to house the Van den Ende Foundation.

❺ Het Tuynhuys★

Reguliersdwarsstraat, 28
☎ 627 66 03
Mon.-Fri. noon-2.30pm, every day 6-10.30pm.

This former coach house, hidden behind the flower market, was designed by the photographer and interior decorator Kees Hageman. In summer you can eat in the beautiful garden to the sound of flute music. The tempting set meals and varied à la carte options change with the season.

❻ Willet-Holthuysen Museum★★

Herengracht, 605
☎ 523 18 22
Mon.-Fri. 10am-5pm, Sat.-Sun. 11am-5pm (closed Jan. 1, Apr. 30 and Dec. 25)
Entrance charge
See Don't Miss p. 78.

The Willet Holthuysens, the couple who owned this lovely 17th-century residence, were avid collectors of glassware, porcelain, silverware and paintings. Experience scenes from the daily life of wealthy 18th-century bourgeois Amsterdammers.

❽ Cinéma Tuschinski★★

Reguliersbreestraat, 26-28
Reservations:
☎ 0 900 202 53 50
www.pathe.nl/tuschinski
Showings every day 12.30-10pm
Entrance charge.

An interesting façade flanked with turrets hides one of Amsterdam's art-deco jewels. This cinema was built in 1921

by Abraham Içek Tuschinski, a Polish Jew who had made his fortune in America. The paneling, windows, lamps and wall-coverings are all original. You can go to see a film (try to get a box in the main cinema), or follow the guided tour lasting 75 mins.

❼ SATURNIO★

A theatrical decor of columns and Moorish mosaics adorns this restaurant, which serves Sicilian cuisine with delicious escalopes and fish specialties. Dishes of the day are chalked up on the blackboard.

Reguliersdwarsstraat, 5 – ☎ 639 01 02 – Every day noon-midnight.

9

200 m

Herenstr.

Leliegracht

Herengracht

Theater Museum 4

Raadhuisstraat 7

Reestraat   Hartenstr.   5 Gasthuis-molenst.

Keizersgracht   Singel

Berenstraat   Wolvenstr.   Herengracht   Spuistraat

Runstraat   6 Huidenstr.

Leidsegracht

Singel   KONINGSPL.

Gouden bocht 2

Leidsestraat   Herengracht   3

Keizersgracht

Banque ABN-AMRO 1

The Herengracht,
untouched
by time

The peaceful Herengracht (Gentlemen's) Canal, lined with magnificent old houses, is the most beautiful in Amsterdam. Its grand residences, whose baroque pediments and severe façades reflect the character of their wealthy former occupants, were designed and decorated by the best artists. To protect the inhabitants' peace, this has always been a strictly residential quarter, and restaurants and cafés are restricted to the intersecting streets. As a result the district has remained untouched by time and you'll find yourself conjuring up the sound of hooves and carriage wheels or the echoes of grand royal parties.

❶ Banque ABN-AMRO★

Vijzelstraat, 66-80.

Yet another illustration of the architectural exuberance that reigned in Amsterdam in the 1920s. This strictly geometrical, multicolored building, 100m (330ft) long and ten stories high, was designed by K. de Bazel.

❷ Katten Kabinet ★★

Herengracht, 497
☎ 626 53 78
www.kattenkabinet.nl
Jun. 28-Aug. 28: Mon.-Fri.
9am-2pm, Sat.-Sun. 1-5pm
Entrance charge.

Cats rule in this fine residence from the Golden Age of the 17th century, with its painted stucco decorations. Not only are they the subject of all the exhibitions held here, but you'll also find live examples curled up in the armchairs or gazing about the garden.

❸ Gouden bocht★★ (Golden Bend)

Herengracht, 507, 495, 475, 476 and 478.

On the curve in the canal, you'll find a group of houses that are among the grandest in Amsterdam. Each one occupies a double plot and their proud, austere façades reflect the wealth and self-assurance of the patricians and merchants of the 18th century.

❹ Theater Museum★★

Herengracht, 168
☎ 551 33 00
Mon.-Fri. 11am-5pm, Sat.-Sun. 1-5pm (closed Jan. 1, Apr. 30 and Dec. 25)
Entrance charge.

Make sure you see the city's finest monumental staircase. It spirals upwards with a false perspective in a hall entirely decorated with stucco and grisaille pictures of mythological themes by Jacob de Wit, an artist much sought-after by the wealthy 18th-century bourgeoisie. The museum's other jewel is a miniature theatre (1781), complete with moving sets.

❻ Pompadour★

Huidenstraat, 12
☎ 623 95 54
Tue.-Sat. 9am-6pm.

Wealthy Amsterdammers descend on this store to buy Pompadour's own luxury cakes, chocolates and sweets. The adjoining tea-house is always packed out in the afternoon, when the ladies take a break from shopping to refresh their energies.

❼ d'Theeboom

Singel, 210
☎ 623 84 20
Mon.-Sat. 6-10pm.

The French owner of this former cheese and butter warehouse is also the chef. The menu varies according to season, with a few musts, such as cinnamon ice cream or ice cream with warm amarena cherries. Sheer delight!

❽ Sauna déco★★

Herengracht, 115

☎ 623 82 15
www.saunadeco.nl
Mon.-Sat. noon-11pm, Sun. 1-6pm.

If you have to work up a sweat, you can at least do it in beautiful surroundings! Every room is decorated with authentic 1920s furnishings. The magnificent stained glass, wood paneling and wall and stair lamps were all bought from a large store in Paris that was undergoing major renovation work.

❺ BRILMUSEUM★

This old building contains a monument to all things optical. You can buy antique frames, or visit the two upper floors that have been turned into a museum. Pince-nez, lorgnettes, optical curiosities, star-spangled or huge retro 1970s glasses, they're all here. Spectacular!

Gasthuismolensteeg, 7 – ☎ 421 24 14
Mon.-Fri. 11.30am-5.30pm, Sat. 11.30am-5pm.

10

200 m

Elandsgracht

Lijnbaansgracht
Looiersgracht
Passeerdersstraat
Passeerdergr.
RAAMPLEIN
Raamstraat
Marnixstraat
Lange
Korte
Leidsekade
LEIDSEPLEIN
Leidsegracht
Molenpad
Prinsengracht
Keizersgracht
Herengracht
Leidsegracht
Leidsestraat
Herengracht
Keizersgracht
Prinsengracht
Kerkstraat
Leidsedwarsstraat
Kleine
Gartmanplantsoen
Leidsekruisstraat
Kleine Lijndaangracht
Prinsengracht
Nieuwe Spiegelstraat
Spiegelgracht
Keizersgracht

The antiques district
and bric-a-brac stalls

As you move from one canal to the next and from street to street, you'll find each is a little world in itself, with its own individual qualities, from the traditional, enduring values of the 80 antique dealers who have been located in Nieuwe Spiegelstraat since the opening of the Rijksmuseum, to the pleasures of the restaurants and theatres around Leidseplein, where there's always something going on, day and night. Between them lies laid-back Prinsengracht, where the antique and bric-a-brac dealers are happy to demonstrate a little originality and a sense of humor.

❶ Couzijn Simon★★
Prinsengracht, 578
☎ 624 76 91
Every day 10am-6pm.

Couzijn has two passions: his bright orange moustache and very rare old toys. This 18th-century chemist's shop, with its floor of polished tiles, is now occupied by dolls with silk hair, rocking horses, sailing boats, dolls' tea-sets and clockwork dogs.

❷ Frans Leidelmeijer★★
Nieuwe Spiegelstraat, 58
☎ 625 46 27
Open by appointment.

Don't hesitate to make an appointment to take a look at the art-nouveau and art-deco

...ecor of what is, indisputably, one of the area's most beautiful antique shops. Frans Leidelmeijer, author of a book on the subject, can tell you all you need to know about furniture and objects designed by Berlage and the Amsterdam School.

❸ Metz & Co★★★

Keizersgracht, 455
(corner of Leidsestraat)
☎ 520 70 20
Mon. 11am-6pm, Tue.-Sat.
9.30am-6pm, Sun. noon-5pm.
Very exclusive and very expensive, this store sells only the top end of the range – and preferably British makes for tableware. All the furniture bears a designer name, like a red and blue zigzag seat by Rietveld. Under the dome (likewise designed by Rietveld) you can brunch on salmon toasties, while enjoying a superb view of Amsterdam.

❹ American Café★★

Leidsekade, 97
☎ 556 30 00
Every day 8am-11pm
Evening meals from 5pm.

With its stained glass windows infusing a golden light, its Tiffany chandeliers and attractive frescoes, this is the most authentic art-deco setting that you'll find in Amsterdam to have a coffee, lunch on a club sandwich or browse through the paper at the big reading table.

❻ Antiques Thom & Lenny Nelis★★

Keizersgracht, 541
☎ 623 15 46
Wed.-Sat. 11am-5pm.

Specializing in antique pharmaceutical items and medical instruments, here are pharmacy chests designed for travel containing carefully packed rows of small phials, some still containing magical unguents. On the shelves are rows of pharmaceutical pots and bottles whose richly decorated labels were painted directly on the glass in the 18th century or on glued paper in the 19th century.

❼ Tribal Design★★★

Nieuwe Spiegelstraat, 52
☎ 421 66 95
Mon.-Sat. 11am-6pm.

You could spend hours examining these multicolored feather ornaments from Brazil, the perfect arc of a bow, the simplicity of African chairs, the purity of the bone objects from New Guinea, the Oceanian masks, the totems, the shields... All the major tribal arts are represented here.

❺ A LA PLANCHA★

Don't worry about the enormous bull's head mounted behind the bar. Perch on one of the high stools to choose from the tapas or grilled prawns in the glass cabinets on the counter. Wash it all down with a Spanish table wine. The temperature rises on Friday and Saturday evenings along with the sound of the guitars.

1ste Looiersdwarsstraat, 15 – ☎ 420 36 33 – 3pm-1am.

11

Overtoom · 1e Constantijn Huyge · Vondelstraat
200 m
Anna van den Vondelstraat
Zandpad
Vossiusstraat
Hooftstraat
Stadhouderskade
Vondelpark
❻
❸
Pieter
Cornelisz.
Van der
Veldestraat
Jan
Van Eeghenlaan
Van Eeghenstraat
Willemsparkweg
Paulus
Potterstraat
Luijkenstraat
Rijksmuseu
❶
Hobbemastr.
**Van Gogh
Museum**
❷
MUSEUMPLEIN
Jacob Obrechtstraat
Jan Willem
Brouwerstraat
CONCERTGEBOUW-
PLEIN
Concertgebouw
❹
❺
MUSEUMPLEIN
Tenlersstr.
J Vermeerstraat
Van Baerlestraat
Metsustraat
Maesstraat
Nicolaas
Frans
Van Mierisstraat
❼

The museum
quarter

No fluorescent haridos or vulgarity in this
residential area with its large, opulent homes
of the heirs to industrial empires. On Van Baerle
and P. C. Hoort, the people dress Italian and eat
French. The only disruption to the orderly streets
is the somewhat anarchic arrangement of the
Van Gogh and Stedelijk museums.

Rembrandt, The Night Watch

❶ Rijksmuseum★★★
(National Museum)

Jan Luijkenstraat, 1
☎ 674 70 00
www.rijksmuseum.nl
Every day 9am-6pm
(closed Jan. 1)
Entrance charge.

During renovation works
(2004–2008), only the Philips
wing with its Asiatic art
collections is open to the
public. Sculptures from
Indonesia, India and China,
Japanese screens and precious
porcelain are arranged around
Bodhisattva Manjushri and the
dancing Shiva. The rooms
on the first floor contain
some 17th-century Golden
Age treasures including
Rembrandt's *The Night Watch*,
paintings by Vermeer and sets
of Delft china.

Rijksmuseum (p. 64)

❷ Van Gogh Museum★★★

Paulus Potterstraat, 7
☎ 570 52 91
www.vangoghmuseum.nl
Every day 10am-6pm
(10pm Fri.); closed Jan. 1.
Entrance charge
See Don't Miss p. 80.

This museum houses the world's most complete collection of this extraordinary and well-loved painter's works. Some 200 paintings and 550 sketches show Van Gogh in all his moods: the somber tones of *The Potato Eaters*, the bright yellows and blues of Provence, and the reds and blacks of his *Wheatfield with Crows*.

❸ Vondelpark★★

1e Constantin Huygenstraat
Every day, 24 hours.

It is no surprise to find that this 45-ha (110-acre) haven of greenery, with its majestic trees, crisp lawns, music kiosk, open-air theatre and numerous water features, attracts a great number of people, whether to do some sort of sport, go for a stroll or simply to have a nap. A stylish café-restaurant, Vertigo, is housed in a 19th-century pavilion along with the art-deco cinema. Don't miss the open-air film shows and free concerts in summer.

❹ Café Welling★

J.W. Brouwersstraat, 32

☎ 662 01 55
Every day 4pm-1am.

The sidewalk behind the Concertgebouw is filled with tables all summer long. This "brown café," has a young and fashionable clientele and the musicians have a special table reserved for themselves.

❺ Concertgebouw★★★

Concertgebouwplein, 2-6
☎ 573 05 73
Every day 10am-7pm.

In 1888 a new concert hall was built on piles at the heart of the new residential districts. The neo-classical façade hides an auditorium with exceptional acoustics, which have given the Concertgebouw its great reputation. It is also famous for its orchestra of early instruments (see p. 130).

❼ Brasserie van Baerle★★

Van Baerlestraat, 158

☎ 679 15 32
Mon.-Fri. noon-11pm,
Sat. 5.30pm-11pm,
Sun. 10am-11pm.

The young-at-heart mingle with music-lovers in this very classy art-deco brasserie. The shady garden is a boon in summer, as are the salads. The menu, with its hint of nouvelle cuisine, changes with the seasons. The most popular place in town for a light lunch or supper.

❻ HOLLANDSCHE MANÈGE★★

Step through the heavy gate and the musky smell of working horses assails your nostrils. Based on the Spanish Riding School in Vienna, the ring has an Imperial box and a metal roof, and is staggeringly large. Riders and horses have trained here since 1882.

Vondelstraat, 140 – ☎ 618 09 42 – Mon. 2-11pm,
Tue.-Fri. 10am-10pm, Sat.-Sun. 10am-6pm (Jul. and
Aug. 6-10pm).

12

Oosterdock

⑥ ⑤ Scheepvaart Museum

IJTunnel

KADIJKSPLEIN

Kattenburgergracht

Hoogte

Nieuwevaart

Entrepotdok ④ Laagte

Entrepotdok

Kadijk

Nieuwe Herengracht

Plantage Parklaan

Plantage

Henri Polaklaan

Plantage Kerklaan

Kadijk

Kadijk

① Burcht van Berlage

Dokkan

Plantage

② Hortus Botanicus

Plantage

③ Artis

Middenlaan

Muidergracht

Muidergracht

Plantage

Sarphatistraat

Mauritskade

⑦ KIT Tropenmuseum

's-Gravesandestraat

Oosterpark

200 m

Plantage,
dreams of
faraway lands

Far from the bustle of the city, elegant villas and shady avenues give this leafy district an unexpected charm. You could forget that you're in Amsterdam if it were not for the distant sounds of the city. It's here that the Amsterdammers encapsulated their dreams of faraway climes with buildings and gardens dedicated to the people and flora of the former colonies of the Dutch East India Company.

① Burcht van Berlage★★★ (Berlage "Fortress")

Henri Polaklaan, 9
☎ 624 11 66
Tue.-Fri. 11am-5pm,
Sun. 1-5pm
Entrance charge.

The headquarters of the union of diamond cutters and merchants is one of the finest buildings by Berlage, who designed it in 1900 in the spirit of socialism. The severity of

the façade, which symbolizes the strength of the workers, contrasts with the light that floods the interior, growing ever more intense as you climb the yellow stairwell, lit by a cascade of multifaceted lamps.

② Hortus Botanicus★★

Plantage Middenlaan, 2A
☎ 625 90 21
www.dehortus.nl
Mon.-Fri. 9am-5pm, Sat.
and Sun. 10am-5pm (9pm
Jul.-Aug., 4pm Dec. and
Jan.); closed Jan. 1, Apr. 30
and Dec. 25
Entrance charge
See Don't Miss p. 81.

The VOC (Dutch East India Company) first set up these wonderful tropical gardens in 1682 to grow medicinal herbs. Exotic plants, such as coffee and spices, were brought from the colonies and slowly

acclimatized in the gardens. Don't miss the orangery, the palm house containing a 400-year-old cycad, and the greenhouses that maintain different climates.

③ Artis★★

Plantage Kerklaan, 40
☎ 523 34 00
Every day 9am-5pm
Entrance charge.

The city's largest park is home to the zoo, whose many inhabitants include big cats, flamingos, polar bears and sea-lions. There's also a reptile house, an aviary with macaws and multicolored parrots and an aquarium with tanks of fresh and salt water, containing over 500 species of fish and marine animals – just like the ocean, only smaller!

④ Entrepotdok★

Entrance on Kadijksplein.
Step through the monumental door of the Entrepotdok, head towards the end of the courtyard on the left-hand side, and along the canal you'll discover an astounding row of 84 warehouses. Each bears the name of a town where the East Indian Company had a trading post, arranged alphabetically. The warehouses have now been converted into flats, offices and restaurants, including the Saudade, which serves a delicious selection of Portuguese food.

⑥ Scheepvaart-museum★★★

Kattenburgerplein, 1
☎ 523 22 22
www.scheepvaart museum.nl
Tue.-Sun. 10am-5pm (Jun.-Sep. also open Mon.; closed Jan. 1, Apr. 30 and Dec. 25)
Entrance charge
See Don't Miss p. 82.
Relive the extraordinary adventures of the brave sailors who set forth across the seven seas, in this seafaring museum housed in the former Admiralty arsenal. The three floors, with displays of models, navigational charts and instruments, retrace the maritime history of the Netherlands. The royal ship,

built in 1816 for King Willem III and decorated with gold leaf, is the star attraction of the exhibition.

⑦ KIT Tropen-museum★★

Linnaeusstraat, 2
☎ 568 82 15
www.tropenmuseum.nl
Every day 10am-5pm (closed Jan. 1, Apr. 30 and Dec. 25)
Entrance charge.
See Don't Miss p. 83.

Beneath the glass dome of this very fine colonial building, you can travel across half the planet in less than an hour, visiting in turn the cacophony of a colorful Bombay street, the bustle of an Arab souk, or the day-to-day life of an African village. You can also find out about different types of music from around the world.

⑤ ABOARD A VOC THREE-MASTER★★

The *Amsterdam*, built in 1990 and moored in front of the arsenal, is a faithful reproduction of a three-master owned by the Dutch East India Company (VOC) in the 18th century. If you go aboard, you'll gain a better understanding of the physical, mental and spiritual strength required by the crew of 300 men, who had to live for months and sometimes years in such a confined space, prey to scurvy and the elements. Not for the faint-hearted.

13

Around
Centraal Station

Although the city of Amsterdam is built on an artificial island, the central station resolutely turns its back on the sea. Yet move away from the torrent of bicycles, trams and pedestrians surging up to the Dam, and you'll find islands covered in warehouses, with battered old craft moored alongside.

Centraal Station

❶ Centraal Station★★

In 1869 this building, 300m (980ft) long and solidly

anchored in the sea by means of 8,687 piles was a real challenge for Cuypers, the architect of the Rijksmuseum. Inside, on platform 2, you'll discover his secret garden, the royal waiting-room and the Eerste Klas restaurant, with its Belle Époque decor (p. 93).

❷ Stedelijk Museum CS★★★

Oosterdokskade, 5
☎ 573 26 56
www.stedelijk.nl
Every day 10am-6pm
Entrance charge.

This dynamic museum of modern and contemporary art is temporarily housed on the second and third floors of the post office tower. The entrance is through a passageway from the central station. The permanent collections are excellent and there are also high-quality temporary exhibitions in this light-filled space. Next, climb to the 11th floor where you will find the very modish restaurant-bar-club 11, offering a wonderful panoramic view of

he city and the futuristic archi-
ecture of the eastern islands.

❸ Stout!★★

Haarlemmerstraat, 73
☎ 616 36 64
Every day 11am-11pm.

The young and hip of the
district head for the chrome
and primary colors of this ultra-
designed restaurant. Stop off
during the day for an espresso
or salad, or come in the evening
to share the "Stout!" platter
with some friends – five starters
and five main dishes for €25
per person. The world cuisine
on offer is simply very good
food, made with seasonal
products and flavors.

❹ Interpolm Amsterdam★★

Prins Hendrikkade, 11
☎ 627 77 50
Mon.-Fri. 9am-6pm,
Sat. 9am-5pm.

Want to find out all about
KC33, Swiss XT or California
Skunk? No they are not
computers, but marijuana
seeds, specially selected to be
grown at home. Here you'll
find the information, advice
and equipment you need to
grow this rather special
but controversial plant
(which, let's not forget, is
almost definitely illegal
back home).

❺ De Spaanse Gevel★ (The Spanish House)

This café at no. 2 Singel, the
canal which encircled the
medieval city, has a lovely
façade dated 1650, a stepped
gable and a coat of arms
showing a wheelbarrow. This
was where the mail left for The
Hague and the great merchant
ships docked for unloading
after passing through the lock.

❻ Café "In't Aepjen"★★★

Zeedijk, 1
☎ 626 84 01
Sun.-Thu. 3pm-1am,
Fri.-Sat. 3pm-2am.

There are only two remaining
houses made from wood in
Amsterdam, and this café is
one of them. Built in 1521, the
façade is original and the

❼ PRINSENEILAND★

This island, far from the
expensive 17th-century
districts and linked to dry land
by elegant drawbridges, used
to be covered in warehouses
and factories that made rope
and tar. When these closed the
squatters moved in. It has now
become a very sought-after
area, with its warehouses
all converted to luxury flats.

decor inside is just as
impressive, with its paintings
and paneling. The café is
decorated with 17th- and
18th-century sculptures and
antique liqueur bottles with
beautiful painted labels.

❽ West Indischehuis★

Haarlemmerstraat, 75.

This 17th-century house with
its pretty façade was once the
headquarters of the
renowned West India
Company (WIC), not to be
confused with its rival, the
VOC (East India Company).
Today it's a municipal hall
and people's university. In
the central courtyard stands a
statue of Peter Stuyvesant,
governor of New Amsterdam
(now New York).

14

Heineken Experience Stadhouderskade

200 m

2e J. van Campenstraat

Quellijnstraat

Doustraat

Ferdinand

Gerard

Albert

Cuypstraat

Hinckstraat

van der Helststraat

1e Jan Steenstraat

Onvert

Sarphatipark

Sarphatipark

Amsteldijk

2e Steenstraat

1e van Wousttraat

Ceintuurbaan

Willibroduusstraat

Ostadestraat

Kulperstraat

Bolstraat

Ceintuurbaan

Van Ostadestraat

Rustenburgerstraat

Karel Dujardinstraat

Lutmastraat

Pieter Aertszstraat

Sint

Van

Coöperatiehof

Talmastr.

Van Wousttraat

Tolstraat

Eigenhaard

SMARAGDPLEIN

Dageraad

P. L. Takstr.

Jozef

Israëlkade

Amst

De Pijp,
the southern districts

Amsterdam has its own immigrants' quarter, located to the south of the 17th-century city. The main residents of this district are from Turkey, Morocco, Surinam and Indonesia. In contrast to some other European capitals, they coexist peacefully with the young Dutch couples who are also drawn to the low-rent social housing schemes. The most successful of these are undoubtedly those designed in the 1920s by architects from the Amsterdam School. Elsewhere narrow streets and cramped houses have earned this district the name "pipe" (pijp).

❶ Heineken Experience★★

Stadhouderskade, 78
corner of F. Bolstraat
☎ 523 96 66
www.heinekenexperience.com
Tue.-Sun. 10am-6pm
(closed Jan. 1 and Dec. 25)
Entrance charge.

The most famous of the Dutch breweries has moved to a more modern factory, but the old building has been converted into a beer museum. It has just been renovated and updated, and offers an inter-active tour of the history of

beer and the Heineken brewery.

A tasting session forms part of the tour.

❷ Marché Albert Cuypmarkt★

Albert Cuypstraat
Mon.-Sat. 10am-4.30pm.

Since 1905 this has been the most frequented, popular and cosmopolitan of the city's markets. It has around three hundred stalls stretching for a mile, selling clothing, fabric by the meter, fish, cheese, flowers, fruit and vegetables, all at very low prices.

❸ De taart van m'n tante★

Ferdinand Bolstraat, 10
☎ 776 46 00
www.detaart.com
Every day 10am-6pm.

It ideas such as a pink tiered cake decorated with sweets, or a cake in the shape of a ladybird make your mouth water, this is the place for you. You can order your cake two weeks in advance via the internet site and come with your friends to eat it at the café. Breakfast is also available, as are savory and fruit tarts, chocolate cakes and the famous Sunday high tea. The five B&B rooms upstairs are furnished like the tea-shop, in a frenzy of pink, kitsch and secondhand furniture (www.cakeundermypillow).

❹ De Peperbol★

Albert Cuypstraat, 150
☎ 673 75 19
Mon.-Sat. 8.30am-5pm.

This tea, spice and sweet shop has slowly metamorphosized into an oriental market. Once you have seen the range of different size mortars, the most diverse and unusual collection of kitchen utensils, stunning spice pots, full collection of essential oils, tea-pots from all over the world, bamboo bells, and more, you might find it hard to leave empty-handed. And don't forget to try a few of the 212 varieties of *snoepjes* (candy).

❺ Dageraad★★★

P. L. Takstraat.

In 1921 a socialist building cooperative asked two architects, M. de Klerk and P. L. Kramer to draw up plans for 350 workers' housing units. The two brick buildings on the corner of P. L. Takstraat sum up the philosophy of the Amsterdam School, which advocated rigor, verticality and color in designs combining utilitarianism with beauty.

❻ Coöperatiehof★

Entrance from Talmastraat.

In the Dutch tradition of the *hof*, a kind of courtyard surrounded by housing for the needy, this symmetrical group is dominated not by a church but by the bell tower of the public library. The books and key on the façade symbolize the emancipation of the working class through knowledge.

❼ Eigenhaard★★

Smaragdplein.

Another remarkable social housing scheme designed by the Amsterdam School for the Eigenhaard (Home) cooperative in 1917. The school and social housing units are all symmetrical in design. This formalism is offset by the use of soft-toned, and in places decorative, brickwork.

Oude Kerk

Building began on Amsterdam's oldest surviving church in 1309, on the site of a small wooden chapel surrounded by a cemetery. Mixing gothic and Renaissance styles, it has developed along with the city. In 1566, Calvinist iconoclasts smashed some of its works of art. Today, although at first glance its interior may look sparse, the decorative elements, constantly evoking the city's seafaring past, are fascinating.

The bell tower

Built in 1565 by Joost Jansz Bilhamer, the Old Church's gothic clock tower was once a landmark for sailors. Today, its 47-bell carillon, added in 1658 by François Hemony, marks the passing of time through the Amsterdammers' day. It is well worth climbing up the tower for the wonderful view of the city.

The exterior

The church's gabled chapels form an interesting contrast with the surrounding red-light district, and the gothic-style north door is particularly worth a look. The various small 17th- and 18th-century buildings and annexes around the church are used by the ecclesiastical administrative authorities.

The interior

The building has a number of treasures, including the pulpit, which dates from 1643, the choir stalls (1681), the big oak organ (1724) by Jan Westerman and, in the Chapel of the Virgin, the magnificent 16th-century stained glass windows by Pieter Aertsen depicting the Immaculate Conception, the Visitation and the Dormition. Major restoration works carried out in 1955 revealed 15th-century paintings on the ceiling. A number of Dutch admirals who died in combat are buried in the sanctuary, and in 1642 Rembrandt's first wife Saskia was interred here near the choir.

INFORMATION

Oude Kerk (see p. 50)
Oude Kerksplein, 23
☎ 625 82 84
www.oudekerk.nl
Mon.-Sat. 11am-5pm,
Sun. 1-5pm
Entrance charge
Sat. 4-5pm, bell-ringing
concerts.

Nieuwe Kerk

By the 15th century, the Oude Kerk (Old Church) had become too small to accommodate all the local worshippers. Construction began on the Nieuwe Kerk (New Church) in 1408 in the flamboyant gothic style. Following several major fires, the new church was revamped a number of times, notably in 1645 by Jacob van Campen, the architect of the Royal Palace. The coronations of the Dutch heads of state have taken place here since 1813, but today it is mainly used for exhibitions, conferences and concerts.

The stained-glass windows

The Nieuwe Kerk has 75 stained glass windows – a feature for which it is rightly famous. The oldest is in the north transept. It depicts Count Willem IV of Holland, and was designed in 1650 by Gerrit Jansz van Bronchorst.

The pulpit

The mahogany pulpit, which was completed in 1664, took Albert Vinckenbrinck 15 years to carve. Its carving depicts the Misericord, the Cardinal Virtues and the Evangelists. An impressive work of art!

The organ

The organ, designed by Jacob van Campen in 1645, is embellished with delightful wooden carvings by Artus Quellijn (the sculptor of the Royal Palace) and paintings by Jan Gerritsz van Bronchorst that depict scenes from the life of David.

The tombs

Some of the most prominent figures in Dutch history lie buried in the Nieuwe Kerk, including a number from the 17th-century Golden Age such as Michiel de Ruyter (1607-1676), a Dutch admiral who died fighting the French at the battle of Messina. Also, look out for the tomb of the greatest Dutch poet, Joost Van den Vondel (1587-1679).

INFORMATION

Nieuwe Kerk (see p. 42)
☎ 626 81 68
www.nieuwekerk.nl
Open during temporary exhibitions
Every day 10am-6pm (10pm Thu.)
Entrance charge.

Amsterdams Historisch Museum

The sculptures, paintings, maps and models in the Historical Museum's collections recount Amsterdam's development from its foundation in the 3rd century to the start of the 20th century. The museum building was originally a 15th-century convent, which became an orphanage in 1581. Temporary exhibitions are organized in the part of the building previously reserved for the orphans.

The 14th and 15th centuries

From the 14th century onwards, the modest fishing village on the banks of the Amstel began to develop into a commercial port. Soon thousands of pilgrims were making their way to the city, after a miracle which took place in a house in the center of Amsterdam: a sacred host thrown into the fire was found intact. This event is depicted in the painting by Jacob Cornelisz van Oostanen entitled *The Miracle of Amsterdam*.

Amsterdam in the 16th century

In Room I, the medieval city is depicted in the smallest detail on the wood carving by Cornelis Anthonisz (1538). The revolt against the Spanish is shown in the portraits of William of Orange and Philip II of Spain.

The Golden Age

Amsterdam's development throughout the 17th century was principally linked to the city's maritime activities. Consequently, there is a whole room devoted to expeditions and voyages of exploration. Look at the models of the East India Company boats.

The Regents' Room

The directors of the orphanage used this room for meetings in the 17th century. It contains furniture dating from the time as well as the regents' arms, portraits and paintings by Abraham de Verwer.

The Gallery of the Civic Guard

This glass-paneled gallery was opened in 1975 and displays group portraits (16th and 17th century) of civic guards. It links the boys' yard to the girls' yard and is open to everyone during the museum's opening hours.

INFORMATION

Amsterdams Historisch Museum (see p. 41)
Kalverstraat, 92
Nz Voorburgwal, 357
☎ 523 18 22
www.ahm.nl
Mon.-Fri. 10am-5pm,
Sat.-Sun. 11am-5pm
Closed Jan. 1, Apr. 30
and Dec. 25
Entrance charge.

Amstelkring
Museum

This house with its pointed gables was built in **1663** by the German merchant Jan Hartman. In the same year, he bought the two neighboring houses and was able to install a hidden church known as Ons' Lieve Heer op Solder ("Our Lord in the Attic") across the three upper floors. In **1888**, the private Amstelkring Foundation renovated the building and turned it into a museum. Services are still held in the church today, and it is also a concert venue.

The drawing room

A very narrow staircase leads up to the first floor. This room contains all the characteristic items of Dutch bourgeois decor from the 17th-century Golden Age: a coffered ceiling, tiled floor and portraits by Jacob de Wit (1695-1754).

The chaplain's room

It is hard to imagine the existence of the priest, who lived secretly in this modest room hidden under the chapel. Some of his personal objects, including spectacles, a breviary, a pipe and some slippers, still remain.

The church

The owner built a chapel dedicated to St Nicholas under the roof of his bourgeois house as a place where Catholics could worship at a time when their religion was outlawed and Protestantism held sway. In 1735, remodeling work began – it was vested with a baroque-style altar in false marble surmounted by a *Baptism of Christ* (1716) by Jacob de Wit, a pulpit, rows of seats and an organ (1794). Services were held here until the Sint Nicolaaskerk was built in 1887. Besides boasting portraits, engravings and statues, the house also displays a collection of silver liturgical objects.

INFORMATION

Amstelkring Museum
(see p. 50)
Oudezijds
Voorburgwal, 40
☎ 624 66 04
www.
museumamstelkring.nl
Mon.-Sat. 10am-5pm,
Sun. 1-5pm
Closed Jan. 1 and
Apr. 30
Entrance charge.

Rembrandthuis

Rembrandt bought this Renaissance-style house in the Jewish quarter of Amsterdam in 1639 for 13,000 florins. This was where he painted many of his major works such as *The Night Watch* (1642), but in 1658, chronic financial difficulties forced him to sell it by auction. In 1998, the house was entirely renovated, decorated and furnished on the basis of Rembrandt's pictures and the inventory of his goods drawn up at the time of the sale. The museum has expanded into the neighboring property, making it possible to display the rich collection of 290 engravings as well as to hold temporary exhibitions.

The ground floor

This was where Rembrandt lived and worked as an art dealer. Pictures by his Dutch and Flemish contemporaries (Pieter Lastman, Geerbrandt van den Eeckout, Rubens, Ferdinand Bol, etc.) hang on the walls. The anterooms – the Voorhuys and the Sijdel-caemer – are where the artist displayed the works and received his clients. Behind the Sijdelcaemer is the room where the artist did his etchings, containing the press, copper plates and tools. The Agtercaemer, furnished with a table, chairs and a box bed, was both the living room and the bedroom.

The basement

Restoration works uncovered objects dating back to Rembrandt's time in the small courtyard behind the house. These include clay pipes, German stoneware jars and Italian china. It may well be in this courtyard that Rembrandt painted *The Night Watch*. The most comfortable room in Rembrandt's house is perhaps the kitchen, tiled in black and white with a wide chimney over the fireplace. The box bed belonged to the maid Hendrickje Stoffels, who was to become the painter's great love five years after the death of his wife Saskia.

INFORMATION

Rembrandthuis
(see p. 52)
Jodenbreestraat, 4-6
☎ 520 04 00
www.rembrandthuis.nl
Mon.-Sat. 10am-5pm
and Sun. 1-5pm
Closed Jan. 1
Entrance charge.

The first floor

The Kunstcaemer is the room where Rembrandt kept his collection of curiosities and is an interesting insight into Rembrandt's multifaceted nature as a remarkable painter, collector and antique dealer. Many of the items on display in this room appear in his paintings or engravings: stuffed animals, busts of Roman emperors, medals, china, and so on. The huge, light studio is where Rembrandt worked with a number of his talented pupils from 1639 to 1658. The smell of turpentine and the oil that was used to bind the ground pigment to the marble floats over the artist's paraphernalia that would have been used to create the theatrical backdrops to the portraits of corporate groups.

The engravings

Rembrandt was as skilled with his engraving tools as he was with a paintbrush. The engravings are displayed in rotation in the mezzanine and attic and are classified under five different themes: genre scenes, self-portraits — including the one with his wife Saskia, nude studies, views of Amsterdam and biblical scenes. The famous engraving *The One Hundred Guilder Print*, which took Rembrandt ten years to complete, takes its name from an anecdote. Apparently 100 guilders is the amount the painter paid at an auction to buy back one of his etchings. After the sale of his house, he never produced another engraving again — the modest house he rented in the Jordaan district was too small to allow him to continue to practice this art at which he had excelled for more than 30 years.

Engraving technique

Rembrandt probably learnt this new technique from his master Pieter Lastman. Engraving first appeared at the start of the 16th century and made it possible to obtain dozens of prints from a single work. Etchings are created by drawing with a needle onto a copper plate coated with a layer of acid-resistant resin. The plate is then immersed in acid, which eats into the etched lines. Once the layer of resin has been removed, the artist may then complete his design by working on the copper directly with an etching needle (for more delicate lines) and a burin (for emphasizing the shadows). He then inks the plate, covers it with a sheet of damp paper and passes it through a press. Rembrandt constantly retouched his plates during the printing process. By varying the amount of ink applied to the etched lines, he could play on the variations of light and dark. The different prints obtained from the same plate bear witness to how he modified his etchings as he went along.

Willet-Holthuysen Museum

This 17th-century patrician house was occupied by Pieter Holthuysen, a wealthy coal-importer, from 1855 onwards. His daughter Sabrina and her husband, Abraham Willet, in turn inherited the house and completely refurnished it in the French style. Sabrina died in 1895, leaving the house and their collections of porcelain, furniture and art to the city of Amsterdam. It opened again as a museum in 1962.

The kitchen

The kitchen, completely restored to how it would have looked in the 18th century, is in the basement. The full reconstruction has reassembled all the original elements including copper utensils, granite sink and tiled floor decorated with exotic birds.

The blue salon

The salon with its blue damask walls was exclusively the preserve of men.

Above the fireplace is a trompe-l'oeil painting of a hunting scene by Jacob de Wit (1695-1754) and porcelain including Chinese vases from the Qing dynasty (1662-1722).

The dining room

Its sumptuous decor features pale silk wall-coverings providing a luminous background for the 275-piece Meissen table service and matching engraved glasses – place settings for 24 people in all.

The collections

An imposing staircase dating from 1740 takes you up to the collections. The silverware collection consists mainly of 16th- and 17th-century pieces. There is an impressive collector's room, set up as it might have been in the 19th century, containing an impressive collection of pictures. Finally, the room displaying the antiquities has been restored in the Dutch Renaissance style.

INFORMATION

Willet-Holthuysen Museum (see p. 59)
Herengracht, 605
☎ 523 18 22
Mon.-Fri. 10am-5pm,
Sat. and Sun. 11am-5pm
Closed Jan. 1, Apr. 30 and Dec. 25
Entrance charge.

Het Schip

Three public housing blocks were built in the Spaarndam district from 1917 to 1921 by the architect **Michel de Klerk**. The most original-looking, intended for workers on the shipyards, was nicknamed Het Schip ("The Ship") due to its triangular shape and soaring central tower. The former post office and two restored apartments house the new museum dedicated to the "Amsterdam School" architectural movement.

The Amsterdam School

The housing act passed in 1901 was aimed at ensuring basic living conditions and provided the impulse for a whole series of public housing construction work financed by post-war cooperatives. Michel de Klerk (1884-1923) was the founder of an expressionist architectural movement that opposed the philosophy of functionalism propounded by Berlage (see p. 12). Klerk rejected the extensive use of steel and glass in favor of more artisanal materials such as brick and wood, which allowed for more interesting variations in color.

The museum

The post office opened on March 12, 1921 and was conceived in the same social spirit as the housing. It is the only interior design by Klerk that has been fully preserved. Careful restoration work has been carried out on the original coat of oil paint and the lavender blue tiles. The wood and cast-iron counters and other fixtures demonstrate an attention to detail that makes this space both functional and beautiful. The telephone booths have double doors to assure privacy and the telephone wires are camouflaged along the lead of the stained glass windows. The multimedia exhibition, *Poste restante*, consists of ten interviews about the work of Michel de Klerk and the achievements of the Amsterdam School, particularly in the Pijp district (see pp. 70-71).

The housing

Two 2-room apartments under the tower have been restored from period documents using the original furniture, painted paper and materials. They provide a clear indication of the architect's Communist-inspired desire to build "palaces for the workers." The kitchen is to the west to profit from the evening light during supper, the sofa is near the fireplace, there is an open view of a garden or park. The structure of the tower is particularly extraordinary!

INFORMATION

Het Schip (see p. 12)
Spaarndammer-
plantsoen, 140
Bus 22 (terminus)
☎ 418 28 85
www.hetschip.nl
Wed., Thu. and Sun.
(May-Aug.: Wed.-Sun.)
2-5pm or by appointment
Closed Jan. 1, Apr. 11,
Apr. 30, May 5, Dec. 25
and 26
Guided tours around the
area on request.

Van Gogh Museum

This museum opened in 1973 and boasts the greatest collection of works by Vincent Van Gogh anywhere in the world, including more than 200 of his paintings and 550 of his drawings. All the different phases of his artistic development are here, from the Dutch period in the autumn of 1883 to summer 1890 in Auvers-sur-Oise. Pictures by Van Gogh's contemporaries Gauguin and Toulouse-Lautrec are also on display.

Vincent's bedroom in Arles

Nuenen

Perhaps the most arresting canvas from the two years that the artist spent in his father's house in the Netherlands (Dec. 1883-Nov. 1885) is *The Potato Eaters* (1885). Van Gogh was inspired to depict peasant lives, and in doing so to highlight the miserable condition of man. In the dark room, the faces and everyday objects are illuminated only by a tiny flame.

Paris

Van Gogh met the impression-ists Monet and Degas when he moved to Paris in 1886.

During this period, he painted landscapes, still lifes, flowers and several self-portraits (including *Self-portrait with Straw Hat*) where the expressive values of his colors intensified considerably.

Arles

This was without a doubt the painter's most productive period: almost 200 paintings and more than 100 drawings between February 1888 and May 1889. The nature that surrounded him became the principal subject of his canvases. The artist rejoiced in the quality of the Provençal light and yellow became the symbol of the faith and hope that inundate pictures such as his famous *Sunflowers* or *Vincent's House* in Arles.

Auvers-sur-Oise

Despite a period at the St-Rémy asylum, Van Gogh's mental health continued to deteriorate. On the advice of his brother, he took refuge with Dr Gachet in Auvers-sur-Oise, but solitude overwhelmed him and a few weeks after having painted such tormented landscapes as *Wheat Field with Crows,* he fatally shot himself.

INFORMATION

Van Gogh Museum
(see p. 65)
Paulus Potterstraat, 7
☎ 570 52 91
www.vangoghmuseum.nl
Every day 10am-6pm
(10pm on Wed.)
Closed Jan 1
Entrance charge.

Hortus Botanicus

A wonderful oasis where you'll find tropical and desert species, a Japanese garden and a winter garden, seasonal flowers and rare plants. There are guided tours on particular themes, such as the many exotic trees that have grown here since the 17th century. You can also get advice on looking after your own plants. If you're lucky, you might catch the giant water lily, *Victoria amazonica,* in flower – but time it carefully as it only blooms for two nights a year!

Medicinal plants and spices

In 1682, a small garden of medicinal herbs founded by the pharmacy faculty in 1638 was moved to the new Plantage district. One of the gardens, the Semicircle, gives an impression of how the garden would have looked originally, with the arrangement by species of clove, cinnamon and nutmeg trees and other spices and exotic plants that the East India Company brought back from the Moluccas, the Indonesian spice islands. Botanists would have carefully selected the most robust plants for introduction into their colonies, such as coffee, tobacco and the oil palm.

The Palm-house

The garden boasts more than 8,000 different species including an extraordinary collection of cycads and a male and female Eastern Cape bread-tree (*Encephalartos altensteinii*), aged 300 and 250 years respectively. Acquired by King Willem II in 1851, they number among the world's oldest pot plants and flowered in the summer of 1999. Most of the big trees were planted in 1895.

The Orangery

The hot-house was built in the 19th century for the wintering of different varieties of citrus, and has been used as a conference hall by the University of Amsterdam and even as an exhibition hall for the collection of 62 species of wild animals owned by Louis Napoleon during his brief reign as king of Holland. Today it is an ideal place for a quiet lunch or cup of tea.

INFORMATION

Hortus Botanicus
(see p. 66)
Plantage Middenlaan, 2A
☎ 625 90 21
www.dehortus.nl
Mon.-Fri. 9am-5pm,
Sat. and Sun. 10am-5pm
(9pm Jul.-Aug., 4pm
Dec.-Jan.)
Closed Jan 1, Apr. 30
and Dec. 25
Entrance charge.

Scheepvaart Museum

Since 1981, the Netherlands Maritime Museum has been housed in a huge building that was formerly the arsenal of the Dutch Navy. The naval depot was built in 1656 by Daniel Stalpaert; it stands on the edge of the Oosterdok dock, and was large enough to store all the provisions required to supply the ships. Dutch navigational history is presented in chronological order through a far-ranging collection of models, instruments, maps, pictures and globes.

Amazing replicas

The Royal Barge on the ground floor was built in 1818 for Willem I. The Amsterdam is a faithful reproduction of an 18th-century three-master owned by the East India Company (VOC) that ran aground on the English coast in 1749. Among the other vessels moored on the jetty in front of the museum is the Balder, a herring lugger dating from 1912, a steam-powered ice-breaker and a life-boat.

Cartography

On the first floor, the *Atlas Blaeu*, by Jan Blaeu (1598–1673) was originally published in Amsterdam in 1663 in 16

volumes for the East India Company. It represents the spectacular explosion in the production of maps in the Netherlands in the 17th century. Another remarkable exhibit is the planisphere dating from 1648 (room 2). Some of the engraving is only approximate, showing regions that were as then unexplored.

Navigational instruments

Everything you can imagine, from the most ancient to the most sophisticated: astrolabes, Jacob's staffs, chronometers, radars, to name but a few. Finally, in room 24, take a

look through the periscope, which gives a 360-degree view over Amsterdam.

INFORMATION

Scheepvaart Museum (see p. 67)
Kattenburgerplein, 1
☎ 523 22 22
www.
scheepvaartmuseum.nl
Tue.-Sun. 10am-5pm
Also open Mon. from Jun. to Sep.
Closed Jan 1, Apr. 30 and Dec. 25
Entrance charge.

KIT Tropenmuseum

This impressive building was built by the architects M. A. and J. Van Nieukerken in 1926 to house the Dutch Colonial Institute. The Museum of the Tropics opened here in 1978. The collections are arranged by continent so you can get a good idea of life in the tropical regions and developing countries through their music, art and religion, as well as some insight into modern-day issues.

Reconstructions

In the central hall, under the glass dome, the streets and interiors of traditional houses have been very successfully reconstructed. In the space of a few hours, you can walk down an Arab street, experience the atmosphere of an African market, a souk or an Indian shanty town and discover an Afghan yurt or a Bedouin tent.

Art exhibits

Some of the most memorable exhibits include the huge Bisj ritual poles from New Guinea, carved from the roots of mangrove trees, the strangely decorated dugouts from the Pacific and the collection of masks from Africa, Asia and Central America.

Kindermuseum

Children aged 6 to 12 can enjoy interesting and ever-changing collections of art objects, theater and movie shows, as well as displays of music and dance.

The voyage continues…

If you would like a souvenir of your trip around the world, there is a gift shop on the ground floor selling hand-crafted products from the countries you have visited. There is also a tropically inspired restaurant.

INFORMATION

KIT Tropenmuseum
(see p. 67)
Linnaeusstraat, 2
☎ 568 82 15
www.tropenmuseum.nl
Every day 10am-5pm
Closed Jan 1, Apr. 30
and Dec. 25
Entrance charge.

Practicalities

Amsterdam is comparatively small, so your main concerns when choosing a hotel will be price and location. Avoid the central station area and the red-light district unless you like noise and unsavory characters. The hotels outside these neighborhoods are easy to get to by tram or taxi, or even on foot, if you aren't too heavily loaded.

Hotels

The luxury hotels have reduced rates at weekends, particularly if you book through a travel agent, although this may mean you don't get such a good room. There are also many very quiet and comfortable hotels near Vondelpark. The (very large) breakfast is usually included in the price (see Rates, p. 85). Low season prices apply from November to the end of April, and also in July and August. You're not usually expected to leave a tip, unless you're staying in a very grand hotel where you should tip messenger boys and chambermaids. Hotels in Amsterdam are classified according to international standards. There's an enormous amount of choice; however, you should remember that a hotel's star rating is based on objective criteria, such as whether or not it has an elevator, or televisions in the rooms. So in the 2- and 3-star categories, you'll find excellent old-style hotels in former patrician houses, where the atmosphere tends to be warmer and more welcoming. These are the hotels we prefer to recommend. In spring (particularly April and May) and in September, you are advised to reserve several weeks in advance, especially if you would like a small old-fashioned hotel with a view of the canal.

Reserving a hotel

These days it's best to plan ahead and pre-book a hotel in Amsterdam. You can reserve a room by phone, fax or e-mail.

FINDING YOUR WAY AROUND

Distances between places in central Amsterdam tend to be quite short. Walking with a tourist map is the best way to get your bearings, but you may want to hop on a tram if it's very cold or raining.

You will need to give your address, phone number and credit card details. You will forfeit the cost of one night's stay if you fail to honor your reservation. You can also call the Amsterdam Reservation Center:

☎ 00 31 20 551 25 25
✆ 00 31 20 201 88 50.
www.res.amsterdamtouriste.nl
This is a central reservation service. You can also e-mail: reservations@atcb.nl
For last minute reservations, contact GWK: ☎ 0 900 05 66. It's worth checking out the websites www.hotels.nl and www.ratestogo.com for special offers and reductions.

Restaurants

Dutch food isn't particularly widely renowned, but the best place to enjoy the hearty, unpretentious cuisine is in an *eetcafé*, where the daily special is often *stoemp*, mashed potato mixed with vegetables or *hutspot*, a meat stew with vegetables. Look out for pea and bacon soup and raw or marinated herrings, which are other specialties. Restaurants displaying the Neerlands Dis logo all serve traditional cuisine. A visit to

Amsterdam would not be complete without a trying a *rijsttafel* in an Indonesian restaurant. Many restaurants are French or Italian and sometimes both. You can also find excellent Thai, Chinese, Japanese and Spanish food. Fashionable establishments and those in a great setting are inevitably more expensive, but this is not necessarily a reflection of the quality of the food. Three restaurants have

been awarded special mentions in the gourmet guides: La Rive, Christophe (see p. 92) and Sichuan Food (see p. 91). Our selections are mostly based on value for money.
In cafés you can often order snacks like a cheese platter, *vlammetjes* or *bitterballen*. *Jenever* (the Dutch version of gin) is the national drink. A late night favourite is "eating out of the wall" in brightly lit snack bars called *febo* where the deep fried snacks are displayed and kept hot in individual vending machines. During the day, you can eat on the street at various fish stalls, where you can try the famous raw herring or other smoked or fried fish. The Dutch like to economize and don't often eat out.

Restaurants are generally the preserve of businessmen and tourists and can be very expensive if you pick from the à la carte menu. For this reason, the great majority of restaurants offer more reasonably priced set meals of between three and five courses. Prices as shown include a 15 percent service charge. The Dutch seldom leave a tip, though they may sometimes round up the bill.

In restaurants, the tip shouldn't be more than €5. Lastly, remember that the Dutch eat early. Restaurants are open from 6pm and the kitchen usually closes at 10pm. A few places around the Concertgebouw, Leidseplein and Rembrandtplein stay open until midnight. However, the most sensible thing is always to call first and book if you don't want to have to resort to McDonald's.

NO PLACE FOR THE WAR ON SMOKING

As yet, there is no antismoking legislation in the Netherlands, which means that there are few restaurants or cafés with no-smoking areas.

Hotels

1 - Canal House
2 - Toro (p.88)
3 - De l'Europe
4 - Prinsenhof

The Dam

Winston★★

Warmoesstraat, 129
☎ 623 13 80
☎ 639 23 08
www.winston.nl

Between the Stock Exchange and the Dam, this cool new hotel attracts guests aged 25-40. Most of the 67 rooms are decorated by Dutch artists. When booking, state whether you want a room with a work of art and en-suite shower – these are €12 more than the rooms with a shared shower. Night-clubbers gather in the bar and the attached nightclub.

Rokin

Agora★★

Singel, 462
☎ 627 22 00
☎ 627 22 02
www.hotelagora.nl

This small, pleasant hotel near the flower market has 16 rooms decorated in art-deco style with modern bathrooms. You can choose between rooms for two to four people and a view of the canal (slightly more expensive) and the quieter rooms at the back. The couple who run it are friendly and welcoming

De l'Europe★★★★★

Nieuwe Doelenstraat, 2-8
☎ 531 17 77
☎ 531 17 78
www.deleurope.nl

This luxury hotel, with its fantastic location in the heart of Amsterdam, was opened in 1896 Famous guests have included Elizabeth Taylor and other American celebrities. The hotel combines refinement with personal service and has an excellent restaurant, the Excelsior, a large waterside terrace, a fitness center with a small, Hollywood-style swimming pool and a private parking lot. Ask for a room with a balcony overlooking the Amstel.

Around Jordaan

Blakes★★★★★

Keizersgracht, 384
☎ 530 20 10
🕿 530 20 30
www.blakesamsterdam.com

The most recent of Amsterdam's stylish hotels is the creation of London designer Anouska Hempel. She has successfully given the historic 17th-century building a very contemporary edge with each of the rooms decorated in a subtly different colors. The excellent restaurant, a secret garden, a private boat and bicycles for the use of guests, are just some of the numerous benefits of this magical and exclusive place.

Toren★★★★

Keizersgracht, 164
☎ 622 63 52
🕿 626 97 05
www.hoteltoren.nl

Located on one of the most beautiful canals, this hotel is

comfortable and welcoming. Ask for a room overlooking either the canal or for the small, Laura-Ashley style house in the garden (room 111). Reductions for stays of more than three nights during the winter. Characterful bar with old woodwork.

Canal House★★★

Keizersgracht, 148
☎ 622 51 82
🕿 624 13 17.

The best-designed of the small, old-style hotels. Intimate 17th-century decor in a beautiful house on the edge of Jordaan. Crystal chandeliers, fresh flowers, period furniture and antiques. Reserve two months in advance.

Acacia★

Lindengracht, 251
☎ 622 14 60
🕿 638 07 48
www.hotelacacia.nl

A small, modest hotel with 14 rooms and a very Dutch feel, run by a young couple, which offers the basic essentials. En-suite bathrooms and a large breakfast included in the price. For something different, try one of the rooms in the hotel's two houseboats on the nearby canal. Reservation essential. Add five percent to the bill for payment by credit card

Rembrandtplein

Seven one Seven★★★★★

Prinsengracht, 717
☎ 427 07 17
🕿 423 07 17
www.717hotel.nl

Enjoy a dream weekend in a luxurious suite in this vast 19th-century patrician mansion on the edge of the Princes' Canal. The intimate atmosphere and the sophisticated decor that

differs subtly in the eight rooms and suites is just the thing for anyone who would like a taste of the rich Amsterdammers' way of life. Breakfast is served in your room or on the two flowery terraces.

Seven Bridges★★★

Reguliersgracht, 31
☎ 623 13 29.

A small eight-room hotel by the most beautiful of the canals whose owner, an antique dealer, has decorated it in a range of styles, from empire to art deco. Vases filled with flowers, Persian carpets and a big breakfast served in bed. Views over the garden or the canal, but the staircase is steep. An excellent hotel where you should reserve at least three weeks In advance for spring or summer.

Prinsenhof★

Prinsengracht, 810
☎ 623 17 72
🕿 638 33 68
www.hotelprinsenhof.com

A small, tastefully decorated hotel near Frederiksplein and the friendly cafés of Utrechtsestraat, which would suit those on limited budgets who don't mind steep stairs. Reserve a long way in advance if you want one of the three rooms with an en-suite shower. There's a five percent surcharge for credit cards.

Around Herengracht

Ambassade★★★

Herengracht, 341
☎ 555 02 22
🕿 555 02 77
www.ambassade-hotel.nl
The favorite hotel of authors Michel Tournier and Umberto Eco, this is the most luxurious of the old-style hotels, occupying

eight fine 17th-century houses. Period furniture and interesting and unusual decor in the public areas. A choice of top-floor bedrooms under the rafters or very large rooms overlooking the canal. So quiet you can hear the ducks quacking. 24-hour restaurant service.

Keizershof★

Keizersgracht, 618
☎ 622 28 55
❶ 624 84 12
www.keizershof.nl

An authentic 17th-century building, where Mrs De Vries makes you feel at home in a typically Dutch setting. Six pleasant rooms with period furniture and old-fashioned linen. In good weather breakfast is served in the flower-filled garden and there is a piano in the lounge.

The museum quarter

Bilderberg Jan Luyken★★★★

Jan Luijkenstraat, 58
☎ 573 07 30
❶ 676 38 41
www.janluyken.nl

In a quiet street near Vondelpark, theatres and museums, the Van Schalk family have turned three 19th-century patrician houses into a hotel. Quiet atmosphere, classic furniture, art-nouveau decor and a warm welcome at an affordable price. It is possible to park in the street, but you have to pay for it.

Toro★★★★

Koningslaan, 64
☎ 673 72 23
❶ 675 00 31
www.ams.nl

This hotel is an old patrician house ten minutes from the center, next to Vondelpark, with 22 comfortable and delightfully quiet rooms. You'll find a breakfast room opening onto the garden, a terrace, antique furniture, oriental carpets and a very warm welcome. There are many parking facilities available in the area. Toro represents excellent value for money.

De Filosoof★★★

Anna van den Vondelstraat, 6
☎ 683 30 13
❶ 685 37 50
www.hotelfilosoof.nl

This hotel near Vondelpark and the cinema museum has an unusual feature – the decor of the 25 rooms is inspired by philosophy. You sleep under the watchful eye of Kant, Goethe, Marx, Dante or one of the great Japanese thinkers. Not that this means a lack of comfort – quite the opposite, in fact. Breakfast in the garden in fine weather. De Filosoof is a high-quality (and high-minded) hotel.

Villa Borgmann★★★

Koningslaan, 48
☎ 673 52 52
❶ 676 25 80.

This small, peaceful and welcoming hotel, situated in the residential area by Vondelpark, has 15 rooms with en-suite showers, the best of which overlook the park. Cane furniture and pastel tones. Parking available nearby.

Plantage

Amstel Intercontinental★★★★★

Prof. Tulplein, 1
☎ 622 60 60
❶ 622 58 08
www.amsterdam.intercontinental.com

This luxury hotel, built in 1867 and restored at great expense, offers its clients a personalized service. The 79 rooms are amazingly sumptuous, boasting upscale furniture, silk sheets, crystal carafes in the bar and a bathroom fit for a film star.

Lloyd Hotel

1 - Lloyd Hotel –
   Restaurant Snel
2 - Amstel Intercontinental
3 - Ambassade (pp. 87-88)

Other features include a manned car-park, heated pool, sauna, Turkish bath, limousines and gourmet restaurant, La Rive, with its terrace along the Amstel.

Around Centraal Station

Lloyd Hotel ★★★★

**Oostelijke Handelskade, 34
(D2/E2 – Bus 43, tram 10)
☎ 419 18 40
🖷 419 18 44
www.lloydhotel.com**

A huge modernist building built in 1918 that was once a transit center for immigrants from Eastern Europe to America. This hotel in a newly fashionable district has been renovated in a stark minimalist style with cultural and artistic emphasis. There are 120 rooms, a cultural service, a "slow-food" restaurant where you can order whatever you want, a fast-food restaurant and a bar open 24 hours a day, an exhibition space for visiting artists, a library and a small grocery store. The price of the rooms, which are all different, ranges from €80 to €300 and depends on facilities (en-suite or shared bathroom) and size. Suites 221 and 222 are soundproof and have been designed to accommodate musicians.

A-Train Hotel ★★

**Prins Hendrikkade, 23
☎ 624 19 42
🖷 622 77 59
www.atrainhotel.com**

Only a stone's throw from the station, this 17th-century building

was entirely renovated in 2003. The 34 rooms are small but pleasant and have all the facilities offered by a large hotel. A special mention for the Old Dutch suite, with its small private courtyard, and the apartment that would be ideal for a couple with kids. Large breakfast and elevator.

De Pijp

Hotel V ★★★

**Victorieplein, 42
Tram 4 (Victorieplein)
☎ 662 32 33
🖷 676 63 98
www.hotelv.nl**

This convivial 24-room hotel is run by three friendly members of the Espinosa family, who greet their guests personally. It is comfortable and unpretentious, the rooms are well lit, the healthy breakfast is served in an attractive room with funky music playing in the background and there is a pleasant garden.

Restaurants

1 - Mamouche (p. 92)
2 - Long Pura
3 - Long Pura

Amsterdammers tend to eat light lunches in an *eetcafé* or snack-bar. As a result, restaurants are often closed at lunch-time but open at 6.30pm, with a second sitting at 8.30pm. The establishments offering a lunch menu are marked with a ⊗ sign.

Near the Beguinage

Kantjil & De Tijger

Spuistraat, 291-293
☎ 620 09 94
Every day from 4.30pm.

A very fashionable Indonesian restaurant, despite unexciting decor. Serves many Javanese specialties, such as the inevitable and very copious *rijsttafel*.

⊗ Haesje Claes

Spuistraat, 275
☎ 624 99 98
Every day noon-midnight.

This restaurant sports the Neerlands Dis sign, indicating a typical Dutch establishment.

Simple food is served in a warm and friendly atmosphere. The *hollandse visbord*, an assortment of herring, mackerel, shrimps and smoked eels, is a house specialty.

Rokin

⊗ Brasserie Harkema★★

Nes, 67
☎ 428 22 22
Sun.-Thu. 11am-11pm,
Fri.-Sat. 11am-midnight,
reservation recommended for dinner.

This former cigarette factory has been decked out in warm tobacco tones, enhanced with bright colors. Offers good, fast service

and high-quality modern-brasserie-style food at a reasonable price (around €30 with wine and dessert). An international wine list, very mixed clientele and a good atmosphere in the evening. Attractive terrace in summer.

Red-light district

Hemelse Modder★★

Oude Waal, 11
☎ 624 32 03
Every day 6-10pm.

Indian, Italian, French and vegetarian dishes, tending towards nouvelle cuisine, are served in a simple setting overlooking the quiet canal. Three-course set meal for around €26. Restaurant run by former squatters who certainly know how to cook. Very popular, so reservations essential.

Jordaan

Bordewijk★★★

Noordermarkt, 7
☎ 624 38 99
Every day except Mon.
7-10.30pm.

High-tech decor and background music, excellent cuisine varying according to what is on sale in the market, with fish and game specialties. Booking essential for this very popular restaurant known for its wines.

Long Pura★★★

Rozengracht, 46-48
☎ 623 89 50
Every day 6-11pm.

Sublime decor of richly colored fabrics through which actor-waiters glide. Serves authentic Balinese cuisine, subtle and delicate, from Makanan Nusantara to stuffed duck with Indonesian spices.

Toscanini★★

Lindengracht, 75
☎ 623 28 13
Every day except Sun.
from 6pm, reservation
recommended.

A converted factory boasting a beautiful interior decor and a female chef. Inexpensive gourmet dishes are cooked using fresh produce, the wine list is interesting and the atmosphere very warm and lively.

Local★

Westerstraat, 136
☎ 423 40 39
Every day 6-10.30pm
(11.30 Fri.-Sat.).

This ultra-hip restaurant consists of two huge tables where diners sit side by side. The specialty is the meat, fish or vegetable kebab served with delicious sauces and salads. There is an excellent but inexpensive menu (€8 to €16 per dish) suitable for anyone happy to eavesdrop on their neighbors' sometimes heated conversations. Not many wines but a wide range of cocktails.

Around Rembrandtplein

Sichuan Food★★★★

Reguliersdwarsstraat, 35
☎ 626 93 27
Every day 5.30-10.30pm.

Authentic Chinese cuisine awarded stars by the gourmet guides. You must try this place, particularly the hot and spicy Sichuan specialties. Ask the owner to suggest a meal for you, but expect to pay highly for it.

Segugio★★★

Utrechtsestraat, 96
☎ 330 15 03
Every day except Sun.
6-11pm, reservation
recommended.

A sophisticated setting where you can enjoy quality Italian cuisine mixing the flavors of Abruzzo and Venice. The menu, which is changed six times a year, offers risotto and pasta dishes that are a little out of the ordinary; it also excels at tasty fish and meat dishes. Big eaters might opt for the five-course chef's menu (€49.50). The impeccable service attracts upscale Amsterdammers, who particularly appreciate the house desserts and the excellent wines selected from among the best Italian producers.

Tempo Doeloe★★

Utrechtsestraat, 75
☎ 625 67 18
Every day except Sun.
6-11.30pm.

You must try the grilled tiger prawns in coconut curry sauce, the most popular dish on the menu. Set meals start at €30 and the menu tells you how spicy each dish will be. If you'd like to try out the hottest ones, and need some advice, just ask!

⊗ Le Pêcheur★★

Reguliersdwarsstraat, 32
☎ 624 31 21
Mon.-Fri. 12-2.30pm and
6-10.30pm, Sat. dinner only.
A fine selection of fish and other seafood cooked the Italian way in a former shed! Sashimi, caviar, oyster and lobster snacks served until 1am. Eat in the garden in summer.

Breitner★★★

Amstel, 212
☎ 627 78 79
Every day except Sun.
6-10.30pm.

Opposite the Muzeiktheater, this classy restaurant along the Amstel is popular with people who come to eat after the show. The young chef Remco Tensen takes his inspiration from classic French cuisine (foie gras, langoustines) when drawing up the seasonal menu. There are two set menus at €34 and €43 and a good list of wines from France, Italy and Spain ensure its popularity with well-to-do Amsterdammers and business-people.

Around Herengracht

Christophe★★★★

Leliegracht, 46
☎ 625 08 07
Tue.-Sat. from 6.30.

Classic cuisine from southwest France, reinvented by French chef Jean-Christophe Royer. Very unusual decor by Dutch designer Paul van den Berg. Excellent wine list.

Dining Eleven★★★

Reestraat, 11
☎ 620 79 68
**Every day except Tue.
6-10pm.**

A single table for diners among the reds, whites and blues of this minimalist restaurant. French nouvelle cuisine revisited by Martin Keus, a very promising chef who has worked in several starred restaurants. The three-course set menu (€37.50) is accompanied by international

wines classed by Liesbeth the wine expert as "light," "rich" or "powerful." Meat, fish and vegetarian dishes are always on the menu, which changes with the seasons. Its value for money make it a very popular place.

Around Leidseplein

Prinsenkelder★★★

Prinsengracht, 438
☎ 422 27 77
Tue.-Sat. from 6pm.

Cellar with an intimate atmosphere and sober black and white decor enlivened by exotic wood and large bouquets of flowers. Generous portions of imaginative Franco-Italian cuisine, accompanied by selected wines from France, Italy, Australia and South Africa. Not to be missed!

⊗ Herengracht★★

Herengracht, 435
☎ 616 24 82
**Sun.-Thu. 11am-1am,
Fri.-Sat. 11am-3am.**

This new, fashionable bar, restaurant and art gallery with a pleasant terrace mixes styles and genres. At lunch-time, late risers, enjoying the breakfast that is served until 3pm, mix with antique-dealers and business-people chatting over a lobster or a sandwich. In the evening, the menu is more eclectic (dishes cost around €18) to meet the needs of a chic clientele.

Museum quarter

⊗ Le Garage★★★

Ruysdaelstraat, 54-56
☎ 679 71 76
**Mon.-Fri. 12-2pm and
6-11pm, Sat.-Sun. 6-11pm.**
A very fashionable venue attracting a very hip crowd, this

is a former garage transformed by the architect of the Stopera. Red benches and mirrors where you can nibble at the slimming menu or try out the few supposedly French, specialties. In short, the food isn't the main attraction. Reservation essential.

⊗ Sama Sebo★★

P. C. Hooftstraat, 27
☎ 662 81 46
**Every day except Sun.
12-10pm.**

Affordable *nasi goreng* and *bami goreng* specialties and 23-dish *rijsttafel* near the Rijksmuseum. Very welcoming with pleasant decor.

Zabar's★★

Van Baerlestraat, 49
☎ 679 88 88
Every day 5pm-midnight.

Pretty interior open to a garden decorated in trompe-l'oeil. Mediterranean cuisine for those with hearty appetites. The choice includes *gazpacho*, *tajines* or *carpaccio* and some delicious desserts. Mixed, but generally younger, clientele.

Mamouche★★

Quellijnstraat, 104
☎ 673 63 61
**Every day except Mon.
6.30-11pm, reservation
recommended.**

Soft light under the openwork ceiling, the scent of rose and jasmine. A small, simple restaurant straight from a town in the Maghreb! The cooks have been inspired by traditional recipes from Tunisia, Algeria and Morocco, and mix the best fresh local products with ingredients from their homelands – argan oil, spices, truffles. The house specialty is fish couscous, but there are numerous other delicious dishes and the menu

1 - Le Garage
2 - Brasserie Harkema
(p. 90)
3 - Zabar's

changes every couple of days. Wonderful desserts, wines from the slopes of the Atlas, a friendly welcome and reasonable prices.

Around Centraal Station

De Silveren Spiegel★★★

Kattengat, 4-6
☎ 624 65 89
Mon.-Sat. 6.30-10.30pm.
Closed Mon. in July.

Candlelit decor in a 17th-century house. A warm welcome and highly inventive cuisine from starter to dessert, created by a gourmet chef who loves good French wines. Very affordable prices for one of Amsterdam's best restaurants. Reservations advisable.

⊗ Eerste Klas★★

Stationsplein, 15
☎ 625 01 31
Every day 8.30am-11pm, dinner 5-10pm.

An oasis of peace amid the hustle and bustle of the station. Next to

the gilded gates of the queen's waiting-room on platform 2B, the Four Seasons Saloon has been transformed into a superb brasserie serving traditional cuisine à la carte. *Fin de siècle* atmosphere.

Southeastern district

⊗ De Kas★★★

Kamerlingh Onneslaan, 3 (tram 9)
☎ 462 45 62
Mon.-Fri. 12-2pm and 6.30-10pm, Sat. 6.30-10pm.

From the garden to the plate … a dream come true for Gert Jan Hageman, the chef at this new restaurant in the refurbished municipal glass-houses (dating from 1926) in the Frankendael park. Diners enjoy natural light even in mid-winter and it is pleasantly warm on summer

evenings. One of the latest fashionable venues where everyone who is anyone comes to eat the organic cuisine based on seasonal vegetables.

BUT ALSO…

A few others you will come across include **Lucius**, the best fish restaurant in Amsterdam (p. 41); **Cirelli**, for its wonderful variety of pasta (p. 51); **Het Tuynhuys** to eat in the garden in summer (p. 59); the Italian cuisine at **Saturnio** (p. 59); excellent French cuisine at **d'Theeboom** (p. 61); and the art-deco brasserie **Van Baerle** (p. 65).

Cafés
and tea-shops

1 - Canal-side terrace
2 - De taart van m'n tante
3 - Caffè Esprit

after 5pm, it attracts a younger, more fashionable clientele during their coffee-breaks or for a quick, budget lunch.

For lunch on a shoestring, you can choose between an *eetcafé* (café-restaurant) offering soup, sandwiches and a dish of the day, or a "brown café" with the traditional *uitsmijter* (egg on toast) and an assortment of beer. Make time in your afternoon schedule to visit a tea-shop where you can enjoy an *appelgebak* (apple cake).

Cafés

Beguinage

Caffè Esprit
Spui, 10A
☎ 622 19 67
Mon.-Sat. 10am-6pm
(11pm Thu.), Sun. 12-6pm.
One of the most popular modern cafés in Amsterdam, it has plenty of natural light and a big terrace. Join the students, celebrities and businesspeople enjoying a salad, hamburger, delicious sandwich, pasta or an espresso break.

Café Luxembourg
Spui, 22-24
☎ 620 62 64
Every day 9am-1am.
Marble, copper and polished wood paneling give the place an intimate feel. Popular with yuppies and advertising people

Rokin

De Blincker
Sint Barberenstraat, 7-9
☎ 627 19 38
Sun.-Thu. 11am-1am,
Fri.-Sat. 11am-3am.

Near the avant-garde theatres, a fashionable bar with high-tech decor and a winter garden. Snacks are available until 9.30pm.

Jordaan

Het Molenpad
Prinsengracht, 653
☎ 625 96 80
Every day noon-1am.

Photographic exhibitions and a highly literary clientele in this lovely "brown café." Try some delicious *bitterballen* (meatballs) with your beer.

Finch

Noordermarkt, 5
☎ 626 24 61
Every day 10am-1am
(3am Sat.).

A pleasant little bistro where regulars come for a glass or two after the Saturday market or to enjoy the dish of the day.

Werck

Prinsengracht, 277
☎ 627 40 79
Every day 11am-1am
(3am Fri.-Sat.).

At the foot of the Westerkerk, a brand new, contemporary space where you can lunch on a shoestring on tapas, sashimi, salad, prawns or pasta. A good place to remember for its fantastic terrace and weekend dance nights with a DJ.

Rembrandtplein

Zushibar

Amstel, 20
☎ 330 68 82
Every day noon-11pm.

A new trend in Japanese snack-bars. You sit at the counter choosing the dishes as they trundle past on a conveyor belt. The price depends on the color of the plate. Choose from sushis, sashimis, gyoza, temaki and miso. Ingredients are ultra-fresh and the bill very reasonable for Japanese food. No smoking.

Around Herengracht

Spanjer & Van Twist

Leliegracht, 60
☎ 639 01 09
Every day 10am-1am.

Café overlooking a lovely shady canal, with tables set up outside as soon as the sun shines. The patrons tend to be young

and resolutely nonconformist. Snacks and light meals served all day.

Museum quarter

't Blauwe Theehuis

Vondelpark, 5
☎ 662 02 54
Sun.-Thu. 9am-1am,
Fri.-Sat. 9am-3am.

A Bauhaus jewel designed by the Baanders brothers. The blue flying saucer that landed in 1928 in the heart of the Vondelpark now houses a café-bar where you can lunch on a sandwich or enjoy a glass or two on the magnificent circular terrace.

Tea-shops

Jordaan

The Pancake Bakery

Prinsengracht, 191
☎ 625 13 33
Every day noon-9.30pm.

If it's generous portions at great prices you're after, here you can choose from 40 kinds of savory and sweet pancakes. There are some unusual combinations of fillings, such as cheese and ginger, alongside traditional

favorites like chocolate. It's always packed, so expect to wait.

Café Pulitzer

Prinsengracht, 315-331
Every day noon-5pm.
A chic eatery where you can have a quick lunch break or just enjoy a cup of tea and a delicious pastry.

Around Herengracht

Greenwoods

Singel, 103
☎ 623 70 71
Mon.-Fri. 9.30am-6pm,
Sat.-Sun. 9.30am-7pm.

If you are the sort of person to be tempted by scones, cheesecake, *appelgebak* topped with chantilly cream and lemon meringue pie, this is just the place for you. A very British feel at tea-time and more relaxed on the terrace in summer.

BUT ALSO...

• The royal chocolates and the divine bavarois at **Pompadour** (p. 61); the pink candy cakes and the good humor at **De taart van m'n tante** (p. 71); the excellent selection of teas and coffees at **De Plantage** (p. 124).
• The gourmet snacks at **Stout !** (p. 69); the salads with a panoramic view at **Metz & Co** (p. 63); the dish of the day and the beers brewed by **De Bekeerde Suster** (p. 47); lunch or tea at the **Café Roux** (p. 49); the unforgettable club sandwiches at the **American Café** (p. 63); the unforgettable specialties of the **A la plancha** (p. 63); **De Waag** with its attractive terrace and buffet (p. 46).

Practicalities

Where to shop on Sundays

You'll find shops open on Sundays in the city center, on Kalverstraat, Damrak, Single, Leidsestraat, around Noorderkerk, as well as in the district known as "negen straatjes," namely the nine shopping streets located between Raadhuisstraat and Leidsegracht. The current trend more or less all across the city is for shops to open from around 12-1pm to 5pm.

FINDING YOUR WAY AROUND

Distances between places in central Amsterdam tend to be quite short. Walking with a tourist map is the best way to get your bearings, but you may want to hop on a tram if it's very cold or raining.

on the first Sunday of the month during the summer season. This is also true of the commercial district around the Rijksmuseum (with antique shops on Nieuwe Spiegelstraat and Van Baerle and P. C. Hooft streets). The big stores (De Bonneterie, Vroom & Dreesmann, Bijenkorf, Hema, etc.) are also open on Sunday afternoons. Lastly, remember that several markets are held on Sundays, including the ones that specialize in contemporary art, bric-a-brac and second-hand goods, antiques and flowers (the flower market is only open in summer, though).

Opening hours

In general shops are open 1-6pm on Monday and from 9-10am to 6pm Tuesday to

Friday. Most have late-night shopping on Thursdays until 9pm, but close earlier on Saturdays, at 5pm. Some branches of the food retail chain Albert Heijn stay open until 8 or 10pm.

How much to pay

Traders are obliged by law to indicate the price of each item, so you won't get any surprises at the checkout –

here are labels on everything. The only traders exempt from this requirement are dealers in secondhand goods and antiques, so you can usually indulge in a bit of haggling when buying from them. But remember, Holland has a long and proud history as a trading nation, so don't expect to get away with reductions of more than 10 or 15% on the original price.

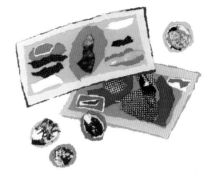

How to pay

Only buy from prosperous and respectable-looking dealers and beware of anything that seems like too much of a bargain. If you're buying a work of art, you can ask for a certificate of authenticity, which the seller is obliged to provide. Generally speaking, you must ensure that you get a receipt for all your purchases. You may be asked to present it at customs and it may be useful should you ever want to resell an item, or when completing your insurance claim if you suffer a burglary. Most shops will accept payment by card, especially Visa, Mastercard and Eurocard, for purchases over €22 or so. For other cards, you should check the stickers on the shop door before you go inside. Eurocheques and traveler's checks are accepted everywhere.

Customs formalities

There are no customs formalities for EU citizens when making purchases, provided you can show a receipt proving that duty on your purchase was paid in the Netherlands. There are no specific regulations in the case of antiques as long as you can produce a certificate of authenticity and a bill made out by the seller.
If you're caught in possession of forged documents, the goods will be confiscated and you'll have to pay a heavy fine. You may also be charged with receiving stolen goods when you get back home. Those who aren't resident in the European Union may be able to get reimbursement of VAT paid on larger purchases, by means of a rather complicated procedure. If you want to do this, ask the seller for a special form (*certificaat van uitvoer* 0B90), which you'll then have to fill in as you leave the country.
For more information, contact the customs office at Schiphol airport on ☎ 406 85 02.

INTERNATIONAL TRANSPORTATION

If you want to ship your new Malaysian wood table home, or that pair of Delftware garden stools you've just treated yourself to, you have the choice of sending them by air, which is quick but expensive, or – if you live in Europe – by road, which will take one to four days depending on how much you're prepared to pay. Here are a few useful addresses in Amsterdam:

Büch B.V. ☎ 696 37 77:
Specializes in the transportation of works of art by road and air.

Hendriks B.V. ☎ 587 81 23:
Road transportation of all types of goods.

Bosman ☎ 020 587 48 11:
Air freight transportation.

Danzas ☎ 020 316 90 00.

Women's fashion

In the past, fashion has not been a priority for women in Amsterdam, who have sought well-made and comfortable garments, preferably in natural fibers. However, independent designers have recently developed original but affordable styles, some eccentric, some smart, while the bright colors and artificial fabrics used in the Dutch ready-to-wear industry are now becoming the norm in younger people's wardrobes.

Sky

Herengracht, 228
☎ 320 00 81
Mon. 1-6pm, Tue.-Fri. 10am-6pm, Sat. 10am-5pm.

Old masters such as Rubens or Van Dyck printed on figure-hugging tops and raw silk scarves, Sherebel de Lilian Konings' designs are cleverly provocative and extremely attractive at a genuinely affordable price (€110 on average). For women aged 30 to 45 and ideally worn with the leather suits (Mansharey) and the elegant accessories under the Mippies label.

The people of the labyrinths

Van Baerlestraat, 42-44
☎ 664 07 79
Mon. 1-6pm, Tue.-Wed. and Fri. 9.30am-6pm, Thu. 9.30am-9pm, Sat. 9.30am-5.30pm, Sun. noon-5pm.

For 20 years, Geert de Rooij and Hans Dermoed, designers trained in Arnhem, have been creating brightly colored garments that have created a stir among people as diverse as Steven Tyles of the group Aerosmith and Elizabeth Taylor. They are all hand-printed on cotton, linen, silk, cashmere and leather. A cool collection of fluid cuts for ladies who need to stand out. Something to suit all tastes and all ages: even your children and husband.

Cotton and linen garments from €200 to €500, leather pieces from €1,100 to €1,485.

Timeless Collection

Prinsenstraat, 26
☎ 638 17 60
Tue.-Sat. 11am-6pm
7pm Thu.).

The shop's decor is as elegant as the clothes, in their sober tones and fine fabrics. The Timeless collection favors silks and natural fibers such as wool, cotton and suede, depending on season. Here you'll find smart suits, simple evening dresses, swimsuits and a wide range of classic shirts and jackets Nothing is very thrilling, but every item is well-designed, sensible, wearable and made in beautiful fabrics. A jacket will cost you €150 to €200.

De Hoed van Tijn

Nieuwe Hoogstraat, 15
☎ 623 27 59
Mon. noon-6pm, Tue.-Fri. 11am-6pm, Sat. 11am-5pm.

Hats off to De Hoed van Tijn, a hat fanatic who has been collecting, designing and making them for 25 years. He produces both classic hats, perfect for Ladies' Day at Ascot

in the company of the British Queen Elizabeth, and totally wild hats for his more theatrical and flamboyant customers. He'll give you your own unique design, made-to-measure in any style you like (one to seven days depending on the style). His hats cost between €90 and €250, plus another €10 for delivery.

M/L Collections

Hartenstraat, 5
☎ 620 12 16
Tue.-Fri. 11am-6pm,
Sat. 10am-5pm.

The ultimate in Dutch ready-to-wear fashions in a high-tech black and white setting. Here you'll find nothing that's too eccentric. Instead the clothes are elegant and lovely to wear, made using natural as well as synthetic fibers. Prices are reasonable and, if you come during the sales, you can get some really fantastic bargains. Jacket €200 to €300, top €50, trousers €160 and skirt €180.

Henk Hendriks Couture

Herengracht, 360
☎ 620 41 96
Tue.-Sat. 11am-5pm.

Designer Henk Hendriks opens his studio to women and sometimes men, creating exclusive, made-to-measure clothes. Designs are made up first in cotton for a perfect fit, after which you'll have to wait two weeks for your unique item to be completed in the fabric and color of your choice. Clothes can be sent anywhere in Europe.

Expect to pay €1,000 for a ready-to-wear suit or dress and €1,500 for made-to-measure clothes.

Demask

Zeedijk, 64
☎ 620 56 03
Mon.-Sat. 10am-7pm
(9pm Thu.), Sun. noon-5pm.

This highly specialized shop comes as quite a surprise. Less extrovert customers might be interested in the lingerie in lacquered leather, while those who want to go the whole hog will like the items featuring chains and nails. There are rubber mini-skirts, long latex gloves and super sexy corsets. The back room contains enough unusual items to waken the devil in even the least imaginative of us.

Hester van Eeghen

Hartenstraat, 37
☎ 626 92 12
Mon. 1-6pm,
Tue.-Sat. 11am-6pm.

There's no two ways about it,
if you want a truly original
handbag, this is the place to
come. Round, square or
triangular, Hester Van
Eeghen puts the fun back
into functionality. While
the designs are Dutch, the
gorgeous colored leather is
Italian and, what is more
they are made in Italy too. To
complete the look, you can buy
a matching wallet, key-ring,
credit-card holder and diary in
the same leather and color –
and why not the shoes, on sale
in the same street, at no. 1?

Cellarrich Connexion

Haarlemmerdijk, 98
☎ 626 55 26
Mon. 1-6pm, Tue.-Fri.
11am-6pm, Sat. 11am-5pm.

It's the price of success – the
four girls who started out
selling leather goods in a cellar
near Prinsengracht have had to
move to a larger shop. They've
kept the same minimalist
decor, though, to show their
creations off to best advantage.
The bags and accessories all
have an amusing touch, on
which their reputation was
originally based – real leather

and fake crocodile skin, knitted
leather pouches and trapezoid
city bags.

Vanilia

Van Baerlestraat, 30
☎ 679 54 49
Mon. noon-6pm, Tue.-Sat.
10am-6pm, Sun. noon-5pm.

Styles from the 1920s and 30s
in colors and cuts to stand
out from the crowd. Lots
of cotton, as well as fluid
synthetic fabrics that are lovely
to wear. The prices are pretty
affordable considering the
shop's chic, expensive location.
Trousers cost around €70,
tops €35 and jackets €110.

Eva Design

Utrechtsestraat, 118
☎ 428 14 43
Haarlemerstraat, 79
☎ 625 69 90
Mon. 1-6pm,
Tue.-Sat. 11am-6pm.

Roomy jackets, coats and suits
in luxurious hand-woven
materials, mixing natural
fibers such as silk, wool and
cotton. The designs, created
from the interweaving of
threads of different colors
and thicknesses, highlight
the beauty of the fabrics.
Comfortable and original
garments (from €300 for
a jacket) with matching

hand-knitted (€60) or felt hats (from €115).

De Petsalon

Hazenstraat, 3
☎ 624 73 85
Tue.-Sat. noon-6pm
or by appointment.

In a city where the bicycle is king it hardly comes as a surprise that there's a shop specializing in helmets made in all kinds of shapes and materials. For real class, you can't go much further than a matching helmet and saddle! This very kitsch shop also offers crazy belts and sunglasses to add the finishing touches to your ultra-cool look.

Female & Partners

Spuistraat, 100
☎ 620 91 52

Tue.-Sat. 11am-6pm
(9pm Thu.), Sun.-Mon.
1-6pm.

Amsterdam's top shop for erotic lingerie for women (and their partners) is not for the shy or faint-hearted. Esther and Ellen are pioneers in their field, offering an entire range of contemporary erotic fashions. The Viva Maria, Undressed and Murray & Vern collections are the best in the genre. The huge tattoo sported by the young woman behind the counter gives an indication of the kind of eccentricities you'll find inside.

Analik

Hartenstraat, 36
☎ 422 05 61
Mon.-Sat. 11am-6pm.

Young Dutch designer Analik has created a line of hip clothing and she's already had her own Paris show, in October 2000. The fabrics all have that feel-good factor, and the lines are distinctly modern and feminine, while practical enough for the busiest lifestyle.

Van Heek Lust for Leather

Lindengracht, 220
☎ 627 07 78
Sat. noon-6pm and by
appointment in the week.

Joyce Van Heek both designs and makes her leather wear for men and women, including lingerie, waistcoats, trousers and skirts, some with daringly gaping laces at the back. There are many designs and sizes to choose from, but you can also have items made-to-measure. If you think you may want to use this service, have some information sent before you leave for Amsterdam. The use of very fine calf-skin (instead

of the more usual lamb-skin) justifies the slightly higher prices (skirt around €180).

Eva Damave

2e Laurierdwarsstraat, 51B
☎ 627 73 25
Wed.-Sat. noon-6pm.

With extravagant little sweaters, woolen skirts and jackets, new colors and original designs, Eva is the knitwear queen. More sophisticated shoppers will particularly like the wonderfully comfortable sweaters embroidered in silk. Spoil yourself, they're not that expensive (around €100 to €150 for a sweater).

WOMEN'S EQUIVALENT CLOTHES SIZES

Metric	36	38	40	42	44	46
UK	8	10	12	14	16	18
US	6	8	10	12	14	16

Most Dutch sizes come up large and you may find you shrink a couple of sizes in ready-to-wear fashion. If you generally wear a metric size 40, you'll probably get into a Dutch 38. If you are having something made-to-measure and adjustments are needed, the shop will take care of it for you. (See also chart on p. 139.)

Men's fashion

For a long time now elegant Dutch men have been sporting Italian fashions, which are well represented in the chic shops of Van Baerlestraat and P. C. Hoofstraat. Dutch men's fashions aren't terribly inventive, with two exceptions – sportswear, which is well-made, practical and reasonably cheap, and the impeccably cut leather wear.

Robin & Rik

Runstraat, 30
☎ 627 89 24
Mon. 2pm-6pm,
Tue.-Sat. 11am-6pm.

All you need to dress in leather from head to toe – trousers, jackets, tops, waistcoats and

caps in different skins. Those who like close-fitting clothes will love it here, especially as Robin and Rik also make made-to-measure garments. Nothing you could really wear to a business meeting, but the effect is guaranteed if you're off to a gay club.

The Shirt Shop

Reguliersdwarstraat, 64
☎ 423 20 88
Every day 1-7pm.

If you're after a classic shirt, don't bother looking in this little shop. Here they're made of satin, velvet or moiré silk, or patterned with spots or checks. In other words – shirts for going clubbing, out on the

town and generally strutting your stuff. The labels are British, Dutch and sometimes Italian and all very cool and exclusive. Try the clubwear shirts for €20 to €40 and the to-die-for printed T-shirts.

Thomas Grogg

Prinsenstraat, 12
☎ 320 16 58
Tue.-Sat. noon-6pm,
Sun. 1-5pm.

The only boutique in the Netherlands selling Scandinavian clothing. Ten designers share the label and offer jeans, T-shirts and shirts, as well as more classic leather or linen jackets. There's definitely something for everyone.

Dockers
Leidsestraat, 11
☎ **638 72 92**
**Tue.-Sat. 9.30am-6pm
(9pm Thu.), Sun.-Mon.
noon-6pm.**

Levi's has designed a new line of jeans, shirts, polo shirts and jackets under the Dockers label. There are more colors and different shapes, twinned with the same comfort and durability that has given this brand its worldwide reputation. American sizes, naturally.

Martijn van Kesteren
Herenstraat, 10
☎ **625 63 71**
**Tue.-Fri. 10.30am-6pm,
Sat. 10.30am-5pm.**

Martijn's philosophy for head-to-toe men's leisure wear is comfortable cuts and good material – linen in summer,

wool and velour in winter. You will always find an essential piece of elegant casual wear at a moderate price among the brands from Germany (Oska), Italy (Rewash) and France (Donovan). This shop is worth visiting for the wide range of colors in both shirts and jackets.

Hoeden M/V
Herengracht, 422
☎ **626 30 38**
**Tue.-Sat. 11am-6pm
(9pm Thu.).**

If you're looking for a real panama hat or a Borsalino, or perhaps a cap or a boater, then hurry along to Marly Vroemen's shop, which specializes in hats for both men and women. A Borsalino will set you back about €130 and can be altered to fit your head in the twinkling of an eye.

Sissy-Boy
Van Baerlestraat, 12
☎ **671 51 74**
Kalverstraat, 199
☎ **638 93 05**
**Tue.-Sat. 10am-6pm
(9pm Thu.), Sun.-Mon.
noon-5pm.**

Don't be put off by the name: this excellent Dutch label creates sporty, contemporary clothes aimed at all 20-30 year old men. The cuts tend to

be fairly conventional, but they're not afraid to use color here, and you can find some more avant-garde styles. The prices are in everyone's range – shirts from €69 to €79, trousers from €79 to €89.

Adrian
Prinsengracht, 130A
☎ **639 03 20**
Tue.-Sat. noon-6pm.

If you dream of finding a really stylish, original shirt, then Adrian's your man. His shirts, to suit both conservative and eccentric tastes, come in fabric of every hue that is chosen in Italy and tailored in London. All you have to do now is match them with jackets and shoes selected with care by the designer himself.

For children

In Amsterdam, they did away with traditional layettes years ago. Here the by-word is imagination, with natural fibers, comfortable clothes and matching accessories. Classic, sporty, cool or hippy child, your only problem is that you're spoilt for choice. To make your children's happiness complete, why not take them to a toyshop as well?

Cheeky

Huidenstraat, 8
☎ 320 02 23
Mon. 1-6pm, Tue.-Sat. 10.30am-6pm,
Sun. 1-5pm.
The first shop in Europe to sell this Argentinean label, it caters for kids aged 0 to 12. Good-quality clothing at a reasonable price, and original designs like the knitted hats with ear-flaps, but particularly classics in bright colors. Our favorites are the big-knit jumpers, the cozy blankets, the checked shirts, the flounced skirts and the cute romper-suits.

Oilily Store

P. C. Hooftstraat, 131-133
☎ 672 33 61
Mon. 1-6pm, Tue.-Fri. 10am-6pm (9pm Thu.), Sat. 10am-5pm, Sun. noon-5pm.
If you've had enough of powder blue and pastel pink,

Oilily has a line of bright, imaginative, colorful clothes, adorned with flowers, hearts, butterflies and checks. They also have a matching range of accessories such as bags, shoes, socks, wooden jewelry and hair clips. Of course, it doesn't come cheap (embroidered T-shirt around €40, sleepsuit €35, dress €100 and matching sets €100).

't Klompenhuisje

Nieuwe Hoogstraat, 9A
☎ 622 81 00
Mon.-Sat. 10am-6pm.

The company started out specializing children's clogs but has since expanded its production to other kinds of shoes, including sandals,

walking boots and smart styles. Expect to pay €10 to €45 for a pair of clogs and €10 to €100 for sandals or shoes – sizes 20 to 35. An attractive shop and a real paradise for children's footwear.

De Beestenwinkel !

Staalstraat, 11
☎ 623 18 05
www.beestenwinkel.nl
Tue.-Fri. 10am-6pm,
Sat. 10am-5pm, Sun.
noon-5pm.

This extraordinary shop on the corner of the street is an Aladdin's cave of toys: wooden toys, puppets and heaps of gorgeous soft toys with realistic, expressive faces that parents will fall in love with and children will long to cuddle. The perfect place to come if you need a gift for a new baby.

CHILDREN'S SIZES

Make sure you check the sizes of children's clothes carefully. As for adult clothes, the articles tend to be cut generously:

0 to 1 yr: 56/74 cm;
1 to 3 yrs: 80/98 cm;
3 to 8 yrs: 104/122 cm.

Teuntje

Haarlemmerdijk, 132
☎ 625 34 32
Mon. 1-6pm, Tue.-Fri.
10am-6pm, Sat. 10am-5pm.

Stocking Danish, Belgian and Dutch brands that you can't find elsewhere, with clothes in cotton and other comfortable fabrics for 0 to 8 year olds. This well-cut, practical clothing comes mostly in browns, dark greens and black. Low prices starting from €4.95.

De Speelmuis

Elandsgracht, 58
☎ 638 53 42
Mon. 1-6pm, Tue.-Fri.
10am-6pm, Sat. 10am-5pm.

Exquisite dolls' houses, full of charming details that will whisk you back to a Lilliputian childhood – a fairy-tale world furnished with miniature sofas, vases, flowers and tables, where adults just seem too big! Some of the more expensive items are really the preserve of specialist dolls' house collectors rather than children. House prices start at €80. They also stock a fine range of wooden toys and spinning tops. De Speelmuis is a paradise for the young and the young-at-heart.

De Kinderfees-twinkel

1e Van der Helststraat, 15
☎ 672 22 15
Mon. 1-6pm,
Tue.-Sat. 10am-6pm.

This shop is a tiny Ali Baba's cave contains everything that children aged two to ten years old could wish for. There are costumes and accessories to turn them into princesses, flamenco dancers, angels, Superman or a character from StarWars, Chinese lanterns,

garlands of flowers, an assortment of plants and colored glasses for laying a sweet little table, sequins... and, of course, a fantastic selection of ideas for presents for their little friends. With prices starting at €0.25, you won't be leaving this shop empty-handed.

Tinker Bell

Spiegelgracht, 10
☎ 625 88 30
Mon. 1-6pm,
Tue.-Sat. 10am-6pm.

Here you'll find wonderful dolls' tea-sets with Delftware decorations, amazing musical boxes, kaleidoscopes, mechanical toys and carousels, not to mention educational games to teach your children all about the planet they inhabit. In short, wonderful toys for children of all ages (from €1.50).

Flowers
and gardens

Amsterdammers are true worshippers of flowers and plants, which they use to decorate their homes, balconies and gardens. It's hard not to be caught up by this passion when you walk past the stalls in the flower market, particularly since the prices are so low and there's such a wealth of choice, especially for plants grown from bulbs. The garden furniture and earthenware pots are also very tempting.

Riviera

Herenstraat, 2-6
☎ 622 76 75
Singel, 457 / Kalvertoren
☎ 422 83 63
Mon. noon-6pm, Tue.-Fri. 9am-6pm, Sat. 9am-5pm, Sun. noon-5pm.

Here you'll find loads of ideas for decorating your garden, as well as the prettiest floral arrangements. Big tea-light lamps (€27.50), candelabras (€65), scented candles, cane armchairs, bronze bowls, teak furniture, and cut-crystal glasses. The end-of-summer sales are good for the teak tables and loungers, as well as the new collection of painted cupboards, glass and wrought-iron lamps.

Jemi

Warmoesstraat, 83A
☎ 625 60 34
bloemen@jemi.nl
Mon.-Fri. 9am-6pm.

The flowers look good enough to eat. This talented florist has made a dream into reality by concocting a series of dishes based on flowers: olives wrapped in red rose petals, steamed salmon in tulips; celery and white rose petal salad; herring with violets, and more. A feast of colors and flavors, but bookings (for groups of at least eight people) must be made a minimum of a week in advance, as this incomparable floral experience has been a run-away success.

Vivaria

2e Jan Steenstraat, 117
☎ 676 46 06

Sun. 9am-8pm, Fri. 9am-
noon and by appointment
the rest of the week.

This amazing shop sells
nothing but terrariums — little
indoor greenhouses in which
you can easily grown ferns,
lichen, moss and wild orchids
that resemble the primeval
forest where all life began.
These tiny decorative gardens
are housed inside panes of glass
set into frames of different
shapes and sizes. They more or
less look after themselves, as
long as you make sure they
have water and light. It's like
having an aquarium without
the fish – although you can
have frogs with bright orange,
yellow or blue markings.

Outras Coisas

Herenstraat, 31
☎ 625 72 81
**Mon. noon-6pm, Tue.-Fri.
10am-6.30pm, Sat. 10am-
5.30pm, Sun. 1-5pm.**

A tiny shop selling all you'd
need to lay a pretty table in the
garden: flowery English china,
old-style porcelain, large
earthenware salad dishes,
silvery glasses, gorgeous Indian
tea-light holders, designer-
name household linen,
unusual candles, kitsch boxes
and perfumed oils. If you need
something to wrap round your
shoulders there are some
magnificent Missoni picnic rugs
(€115 to €330) and others
from South Africa. Lots of
decorative ideas for outdoors

and in, with a stock that
changes constantly with the
seasons. One of the small
secret gardens of the "negen
straatjes" district.

Flower market

Amstelveld
Prinsengracht, tram 4.

Less well-known than the
floating market of Singel, this
charming flower market is held
on Monday mornings on the
shady Amstelveld square, near a
wooden church. Stalls stacked
with cut flowers intermingled
with those selling indoor or
garden plants.

Kees Bevaart

Singel (in front of 508)
☎ 625 82 82
**Mon.-Sat. 9am-5pm,
Sun. 10am-5pm.**

Of all the stalls in the floating
market, this is the best stocked
with hardy and seasonal plants.
Here you'll find plant varieties
you may never have seen before,

as well as good advice on how
to grow them.

Firma Straats

Singel (in front of 500)
☎ 625 45 71
Every day 9am-5pm.

The place for tulips and offering
a considerable choice including
the famous black Queen of the
Night variety. There are also
500 different sorts of bulb,
including narcissus, daffodils,
dahlias, hyacinths, freesias,
lilies, begonias, amaryllis, etc.
If you don't know what you're
looking for, they will be happy
to suggest something. Ten tulip
bulbs cost €3.50.

Van Zoomeren

Singel (in front of 526)

☎ 624 39 31
Every day 7am-5.30pm.

This floating shop contains
thousands of varieties of
cactuses and extraordinary
carnivorous plants – best not
to give them a stroke! Just the
place if you want to get rid of
flying insects in a natural way,
or if you're too lazy to do
much in the way of plant care
(cactuses require very little
attention). The biggest
selection of plants and seeds
(2,000 different types) is
available towards the end of
March. The assistants will be
happy to advise.

GROWING BULBS

Bulbs for planting are sold from June to the end of
December. If the winter has been hard, bulbs won't
be available before the end of June at the earliest.
Bulbs planted in the autumn will flower in spring,
whereas those planted in spring (such as begonias,
lilies and dahlias) will flower in autumn. If you have
a heavy, clay soil, lighten it with sand and peat
(see also p.18).

Jewelry
and ethnic goods

As well as the diamond trade, solidly established in Amsterdam since the 17th century, there are a number of shops and galleries specializing in ethnic goods. From magnificent jewelry in silver and coral, to masks from Africa and the Pacific and traditional earthenware crockery, each item reflects a different culture or part of the world.

Hans Appenzeller

Grimburgwal, 1
☎ 626 82 18
Tue.-Sat. 11am-5.30pm.

For 30 years, Hans Appenzeller has created sophisticated, contemporary jewelry, taking his inspiration both from nature and the industrial world. His rings resemble unfurling flower stems, or evoke the undulating contours of an orchid, with a pearl nestling at its heart. His necklaces, on the other hand, appear to have been fashioned from pieces of linked metal that have grown together of their own accord.

Jorge Cohen Edelsmid

Singel, 414
☎ 623 86 46
Tue.-Fri. 10am-6pm,
Sat. 11am-6pm.

The unique pieces created in this workshop are inspired by art deco and the themes of the Amsterdam School. Made exclusively from fragments of old jewelry found in flea markets, from glass, semi-precious stones, Lalique glass, shellac, paste, enamel and silver, these jewels become earrings (from €95), brooches (from €50), bracelets, pendants and necklaces. Tiny originals that are sure to draw jealous glances!

Aboriginal Art & Instruments

Paleisstraat, 137
☎ 423 13 33
Tue.-Sat. noon-6pm,
Sun. 2pm-6pm.

Have you heard the solemn noise of a *didjeridu*? This long trumpet made from eucalyptus branches hollowed out by termites accompanies the ritual chants of the Australian Aborigines. Apart from a wide range of these musical instruments (in wood and PVC), priced between €99 and €800, depending on size and quality, you can buy paintings on canvas or bark by the best contemporary artists. A journey through the "Dream Time" that you can take home with you in the form of a CD or by becoming a *didjeridu* player.

Kashba

Staalstraat, 6
☎ 623 55 64
Mon.-Sat. 11am-6pm.

This pretty shop contains the finds of an indefatigable traveler gathered in the course of his trips across the steppes of Central Asia and the Indian subcontinent. Here you'll find furniture from Rajasthan and southern India, including carved doors and lintels, as well as ikat cloth and items of jewelry combining silver,

KASHBA

turquoise, coral and lapis lazuli. The high quality of these objects is reflected in the prices.

Gallery Steimer

Reestraat, 25
☎ 624 42 20
Tue.-Fri. 11am-6pm,
Sat. 11am-5pm.

This artisan jewelry maker creates classic, timeless pieces

full of invention. He draws the majority of his ideas from the past. If you'd like to wear jewels like those worn by Queen Nefertiti or a bracelet to make you feel like a Celtic princess or Roman goddess, then Klaus Steimer will fulfill all your dreams. By cleverly combining gold, silver and semi-precious stones, he produces jewelry in antique styles, which he interprets with imagination to give them a contemporary feel. You can also have jewelry of your choice made to order.

Bonebakker & Zoon

Rokin, 88-90
☎ 623 22 94
Mon.-Fri. 10am-5.30pm,
Sat. 10am-5pm; open
1st Sun. of the month
noon-5pm.

This jeweler has supplied beautiful items to kings and princes since 1792, and all his products are strictly top of the

range. It's worth having a look at the window display, although there's nothing frivolous – this is serious stuff. Although the diamonds are no longer cut on the premises, they're mounted in superb settings, as are other precious stones. Certificates are provided for all items (the gold is 18 carat). The service and quality are worthy of royalty – with prices to match.

African Art Gallery

Kerkstraat, 143
☎ 06 28 17 71 97
Mon. Sat. 1-5pm or by
appointment.

Walter Lechner is a musician, sculptor and collector of *objets d'art*. From Nok earthenware to Dogon horsemen and Luba neck-rests, all of Africa is represented through high-quality pieces, most of which have come from private collections. There is a vast choice including fantastic works by the Afro-American painter Melvin Clark. A certificate of authenticity comes with each object.

ADVICE ON BUYING JEWELRY

In Holland every piece of gold or silver jewelry is stamped with an authenticating mark awarded by Gouda. This varies according to the number of carats (for 18-carat gold it's a tulip). In the case of ethnic jewelry, on the other hand, there are no marks guaranteeing silver content or the authenticity of amber. A word of advice: Amber is very rare and expensive. It has electrostatic qualities and gives off a slight scent when rubbed, for example, if the beads in a necklace are rubbed against each other.

Novelty stores

In this village-like city, you have to make an effort to stand out from your neighbors. Recent times have seen the opening of a great many novelty stores, specializing in surprising and sometimes bizarre goods. Most of these are in Jordaan and beyond Prinsengracht. Now you have the chance to explore them.

Christmas Palace
Singel, 508
☎ **421 01 55**
Every day 10am-6pm.

Beat the last-minute rush by calmly choosing your Christmas decorations here. Angels, garlands, gilded candles, paper napkins decorated with stars, Christmas trees, Father Christmases and even a special edition of Delftware for your Christmas dinner table – in other words, everything you need to prepare for the festive season to the sound of carols and Christmas songs, all year round.

Marañon
Singel, 488-490
☎ **622 59 38**
Mon.-Fri. 9.30am-5.30pm,
Sat. 9am-6pm, Sun. 10am-5.30pm.

With a range of 150 hammocks from South America, you're sure to find just the one to suit you. Indoor hammocks in cotton and sisal, outdoor versions in hemp, and a variety of sizes, from 3m to 6m (10ft to 20ft) and various weights, from light to heavy canvas, for one or two people. Prices range from around €40 for a net hammock to €900 to €1,250 for one that is hand-embroidered.

Tangam
Herenstraat, 9
☎ **624 42 86**
Mon. noon-6pm, Tue.-Sat. 11am-6pm, Sun. 2pm-5pm.

This is a great place to stock up on lots of small gifts that won't break the bank (average price around €2.25). Check out the lamps, truly original creations that look like luminous garlands of shells, or maybe the unique lightbulbs, decorated in silicon with colored glass balls inside. Guaranteed to give your house a very special glow.

Juggle Store
Staalstraat, 3
☎ 420 19 80
Tue.-Sat. noon-5pm.

Just the shop for anyone who's ever felt the urge to run away with the circus! Whether you fancy yourself on the monocycles (€165), or reckon you could handle balls, skittles, rings or plates in a juggling display, this is the place for you. Impress your friends with your skill with the *bois maori* (€19) – set light to the long ribbons and describe some sensational shapes in the air. David Marchant and Anne van Raaij, street jugglers since 1982, will show you how to handle all these accessories, including the "Plofbal," which is their own invention.

La Botanica
Haarlemmerstraat, 109
☎ 622 29 17
www.labotanica.net
Tue.-Fri. 1-5pm or by appointment.

Whether you want to win back a lost love, rid yourself of bad karma or deflect harmful waves, Azito, a genuine *santero*, initiated in Cuba, can provide the solution with the help of amulets, magic herbs, incenses, powders and scented candles or through a tarot-card reading. In this little corner of the Caribbean where *orishas* (African gods) and Catholic saints live side by side, among their symbols, pearls and colors, you will find all the ingredients to open up paths that you might never previously have considered.

Zinne & Minne
Wolvenstraat, 14
☎ 330 34 82
www.zinneminne.com
Tue.-Sat. 11am-6pm.

Zinne and Minne is the temple of love and eroticism in Amsterdam. Everything is in the best possible taste, and the fact that it sells nine varieties of Kama Sutra "Love Oils," a suggestive tea-service, jewelry, lingerie and a thousand other sensual items does not render it brash or in-your-face.

Fun Frames
2e Egelantiersstraat, 14
☎ 639 39 02
Tue.-Fri. 11am-6pm,
Sat. 11am-5pm.

This tiny shop specializing in ornate and unusual picture frames has recently opened in the heart of Jordaan. From the smallest (2 x 3cm/0.75 x 1in) to the largest (20 x 30cm/8 x 12in), the plainest to the wildest, you can't accuse the frame designers from Holland and elsewhere of lacking imagination. Frames made from driftwood, hand-painted wood, metal, decorated with angels or shells, from €2.25 to €90.75.

Lush
Kalverstraat, 98
☎ 330 63 76
Tue.-Sat. 10am-6pm
(9pm Thu.), Sun.-Mon.
noon-6pm.

Despite appearances, nothing on display in this shop is actually edible. The long multicolored cakes are actually made from soap, deodorant or solid shampoo, created from amazing fresh, natural ingredients, such as the coffee bubble-bath. Best of all is the self-service, refrigerated "salad-bar," displaying the body, face and foot cream. Just help yourself – with a spoon!

SEE ALSO...

Condomerie het Gulden Vlies
Warmoesstraat, 141
☎ 627 41 74 (see p. 51).
All types of condom.

Coppenhagen, 1001 kralen
Rozengracht, 54
☎ 624 36 81 (see p. 54).
Hundreds of tiny glass beads for home jewelry making.

Interior
design

Gerrit Rietveld, one of the major exponents of the De Stijl movement, came to fame with his zigzag chair, which could be easily mass-produced. Today's Dutch designers are just as creative, producing imaginative designs for furniture and lighting. Japanese furniture and exotic accessories match their strict, simple shapes to perfection.

Decor

Prinsengracht, 12
☎ 639 24 42
Mon. 10am-3pm,
Sat. 11am-5pm or by
appointment.

Decor is best known for its range of sofas, which contrast baroque lines with contemporary black and white striped fabrics. Early 20th century antiques and curios, such as the metal latticework

lockers, are merely there to set the scene, but they'll give you up-to-the minute ideas for decorating your home at affordable prices.

Post Amsterdam

Oosterdokskade, 5
☎ 421 10 33
Mon.-Sat. 11am-5pm,
Sun. noon-5pm.

The 9th and 10th floors of the former post office tower are now a mecca of design – namely, the Pakhuis gallery. Against this minimalist backdrop all the latest trends in European (mainly Dutch) design and interior design are displayed. People come here to discover the latest in furniture, lights, material and carpets, to compare and order, but not to buy, as transactions are carried out directly with the specialist stores.

The Frozen Fountain

Prinsengracht, 629-645
☎ 622 93 75
Mon. 1-6pm, Tue.-Fri.
10am-6pm, Sat. 10am-5pm.

A new exhibition is held every month in this gallery/shop, showcasing the latest creations by talented young Dutch designers. From decorative items to made-to-measure furniture, you'll always find plenty of ideas and often ideal gifts to take home. Prices vary greatly, from €5 to €4,599. A hairdresser and stylist recently moved in, so you can make practical use of your time while you contemplate all these beautiful objects. A superb shop that absolutely should not be missed.

Koot

Raadhuisstraat, 55
☎ 626 48 30
Tue.-Fri. 10am-6pm (9pm Thu.), Sat.-Sun. 10am-5pm.

The new art of living Dutch-style, interpreted in lamps and objects created by great designers, including the fashionable Jan des Bouvrie, Rob Eekhardt, Maroeska Metz and Anet van Egmond. Wide range of prices from €5 to €535.

Klamboe Unlimited

Prinsengracht, 232
☎ 622 94 92
Wed.-Fri. 11am-6pm, Sat. noon-5pm.

In the heat of summer, what better than a stylish net draped around your bed to keep mosquitoes at bay? Here you'll find every imaginable kind of mosquito net or *klamboe*. They come on round or rectangular frames and are made of nylon, light cotton or polyester. Prices from €39 to €69 for large mosquito nets and €19 to €29 for a travelers' version.

Fanous Ramadan

Runstraat, 33
☎ 423 23 50
Every day noon-6pm.

A *fanous ramadan* is an Egyptian lamp which is lit on the very last evening of Ramadan. This little shop, on the corner of Runstraat and Prinsengracht, specializes in every kind of oriental lamp,

including lamps made from glass, metal and copper. Here you'll find the rarest so you can recreate the atmosphere of *A Thousand and One Nights* in your own home.

Mobilia Woonstudio

Utrechtsestraat, 62-64
☎ 622 90 75
Tue.-Fri. 10am-5.30pm (9pm Thu.), Sat. 10am-5pm.

The Dutch design shop set out over four floors. Among the classics that haven't changed since 1920 is the famous 201 Gispen ergonomic chair (€455) designed by W. H. Gispen, the clapperboard bed by Martin Visser, the leather loose-cover Chaplin chair (€1,030) by Gerard van den Berg and Rob Eckhardt's "Garni chair." The lighting is not to be ignored either, with the astonishing "melkfles" (bottle of milk) light fitting and the conical standard lamps. Prices start at €20.

Dom

Spuistraat, 281A-C
☎ 428 55 44
Mon-Sat. 11am-8pm (9pm Thu.), Sun. 1-8pm.

Dom is the Dutch for "domicile," or home – and this store is where you will get to preview all the latest trends

in home décor and design at fantastic prices. The sales assistants might be a bit scatty, and some of the articles are ultra-kitsch or downright deranged like the flying cow (€12) and the coat hanger in the shape of a flashy hunting trophy (€7.50). This mix of color, plastic, eccentricity and the unexpected is definitely worth seeing – brighten up your life!

GETTING IT HOME

If you can't resist an item of furniture that's just too cumbersome to take home with you, then try a local shipping company (see addresses, p. 97). Standards for lighting are the same in Holland as in the UK. Items may need adapting for use in other countries.

Exploring
the markets

The way to explore a city's character is through its markets. Among the stalls, from the environmentally friendly to the more highbrow, you'll discover the true nature of Amsterdam. Best of all are the flower and flea markets, where you'll find everything in a very cosmopolitan atmosphere.

Flower market

Singel
Every day in summer, 8am-5.30pm, closed Sun. in winter.

No way you could miss this market, which is centrally located and colorful all year.

Flea market

Waterlooplein
Mon.-Sat. 9am-5pm.

Amsterdam's biggest flea market specializes in second-hand clothes. Depending on your imagination and dressmaking skills, you should be able to dress yourself for next to nothing. What's more, as any designer will tell you, the best ideas come from flea markets. You'll also find shoes, books, CDs and records, old post-cards and army surplus,

as well as stalls selling Indonesian cloth and Indian jewelry, some of which is very beautiful and hard to find elsewhere. Be aware that drug dealers and pickpockets operate in the area.

Stamp market (Postzegelsmarkt)

Nieuwezijds Voorburgwal (Spui)
Wed. and Sat. 1-6pm.

A stamp and old coin market is held twice a week opposite the Amsterdams Historisch Museum. Philatelists and coin collectors are sure to find something of interest here, and business is conducted in a very professional atmosphere.

Secondhand book market

Oudemanhuispoort
Muntplein
Mon.-Sat. 11am-5pm.

In a delightfully picturesque 18th-century passageway

Among the stalls selling farm produce you're likely to find chicks and homing pigeons, as well as more exotic birds – a great place to bring children for a quick natural history lesson! It's also very popular with the residents of Jordaan, who flock to the cafés in the square when they've finished doing their shopping.

Albert Cuypmarkt general market

Albert Cuypstraat
Trams 4, 16, 24, 25
Mon.-Sat. 9am-5pm.

The busiest and most popular of the city's markets. A very cosmopolitan crowd rubs shoulders among the stalls selling fish, poultry, fruit and vegetables, spices, cheese, cheap clothes, pots and pans and leather goods.

between Kloveniersburgwal and Oudezijds Voorburgwal, you'll find stalls selling books for collectors as well as old engravings. Take the time to explore. The Dutch are very good linguists and you'll find books in many languages, including plenty in English. You might also find original engravings of facsimile reproductions of 17th-, 18th- and 19th-century Amsterdam landscapes. All in all, lots of interesting souvenirs that won't be hard to carry home.

Art market (Kunstmarkt)

Spui
Trams 1, 2, 5, 11
Mar.-Dec.: Sun. 9am-6pm.

You'll find good and bad in this market, where many contemporary artists regularly come to sell their work, including raku pottery, watercolors, sculpture and oil paintings. One excellent engraver, Wim van der Meij, sells originals from €29.50

each. Where paintings are concerned, it's all a matter of taste, but what you see here often compares very favorably with the contemporary art shown in galleries.

Book market (Boekenmarkt)

Spui
Trams 1, 2, 5, 11
Fri. 10am-6pm.

Poets read their verses aloud against the distinguished background accompaniment of harp music, while lovers of old books and collectors of rarities rifle through the piles of old leather-bound volumes looking for special editions. A fascinating market, and one that's very typical of Amsterdam.

Farm produce and bird market

Noordermarkt
Jordaan
Sat. 9am-5pm, 4pm in winter.

A lovely market, where ordinary Amsterdammers come to shop.

Bric-a-brac market

Nieuwmarkt
Subway: Nieuwmarkt
May-Sep.: Sun. 9am-5pm.

A very disparate collection of items, from household objects to well-thumbed books and furniture on the verge of collapse. In other words, the ideal place to go rummaging, if you like that kind of thing. There's loads of choice but you wouldn't want to hurry. There are a few new items to be had if you get there early, particularly silverware, ceramics and glass, though ultimately it's not that cheap.

Tableware
and fabrics

Rare, beautiful and amusing objects from all over the world, particularly Asia, and fabrics in brilliant colors, for simple – or elaborate – decorations for your home and table. Amsterdam has many shops selling fabrics you won't find easily elsewhere, but for a few years now high-tech decoration has been all the rage in Jordaan's shops, which keep a close eye on new fashion trends.

Kitsch Kitchen

Rozengracht, 8
☎ 428 49 69
Mon.-Sat. 10am-6pm.

There's no need to go all the way to Mexico for amusing, brightly-colored, kitsch and very plastic household equipment – there's loads of it here. Fluorescent brooms, Corna plates, floral waxed table-cloths and shopping bags, tequila glasses, braziers, ex-votos for Our Lady of Guadeloupe, *piñatas*, Formica tables and an entire department of kitsch toys for your kids. The locals love it.

Rams

Utrechtsestraat, 120
☎ 420 45 85
Mon. 1-6pm,
Tue.-Sat. 11am-6pm.

This highly individual shop sells hand-woven silk, in the form of throws, cushions, table-cloths and nets, against an oriental backdrop. A mixture of ethnic designs, raw materials, colored glasses and the pure lines of old Chinese and Indonesian furniture, all aimed at creating a soothing environment. The price of a 270 x 240cm (9ft x 8ft) throw starts at €134, a 44 x 44cm (17 x 17in) cushion at €22.

What's Cooking

Reestraat, 16
☎ 427 06 30
Every day 11am-6pm.

Specializing in culinary delights, the first and second floors are devoted to all things blue and green, while the basement contains only reds, oranges and yellows. The idea is to fill a bowl with dry goods and sauces of all one color to make a fun, original gift.

Rams (p. 116)

De Hal

Albert Cuypstraat, 224A
☎ 679 59 73
**Mon.-Fri. 9.30am-5.30pm,
Sat. 9.30am-5pm.**

Fabric world! Miles of
imitation cow or leopard,
synthetic fur, organdie,
embroidered silk, cashmere,
merinos, velour, brocade,
goffered fabric, tarin, pongee,
percale, satin, tulle, muslin –
enough to make your head
spin. There are also *Vogue*
catalogues, to give you some
ideas before you order that
Paco Rabanne plastic fabric,
the Yves Saint Laurent lace or
those Ungaro appliqués. To cap
it all, you will get a 10 percent
reduction when you show the
manager this guide, so make
the most of it!

Den Haan &
Wagenmakers

**Nieuwezijds Voorburgwal,
97**
☎ 620 25 25
**www.dutchquilts.com
Fri.-Sat. 10am-5pm, Sun.
1-5pm.**
An essential stop for
patchwork lovers. For
15 years, De Hann &
Wagenmakers have been
producing their own
collection of fabrics for
patchwork, and you won't
find them anywhere else.

Besides a pile of books and
magazines on the subject, you
can get a do-it-yourself kit or
buy something ready made.

Mc Lennan's
Puresilk

Hartenstraat, 22
☎ 622 76 93
**www.puresilk.nl
Mon. 1-6pm,
Tue.-Fri. 10.30am-6pm,
Sat. 10.30am-5.30pm.**

Step into the enticing world of
the finest silks selected from
workshops in China, Thailand
and Vietnam. You'll find them

stretched across the walls or
hanging overhead like
colorful banners. Raw,
smooth, goffered, brocaded,
satin, printed and plain, this is
where the Dutch couturiers
come to stock up with crêpe
de chine, shantung, taffeta
and silk brocade. Expect to
pay €22 to €27 per meter for
a light crêpe de chine and
€49 to €68 for a heavier
example. Truly magnificent
materials and colors.

Studio Bazar

Reguliersdwarsstraat, 60-62
☎ 622 08 30
**Mon. noon-6pm, Tue.-Sat.
10am-6pm (9pm Thu.).**

Despite the somewhat off-
putting "warehouse" layout of
this shop, it's here you'll find
the best lines in crockery, table
linens and kitchen utensils
with a real contemporary feel.
From the most sophisticated of
indispensable kitchen gadgets,
you navigate between the
espresso machines and top-of-
the-range mixers, passing en
route Screwpull corkscrews,
Mickey Mouse kettles, bubble
glasses, a mushroom brush,
pincers for removing bones,
latex chocolate moulds,
"Venus" cocktail sticks and
colored crockery.

BUYING FABRIC

Fabrics don't come in standard widths. At Hotshop,
1.5m (5ft) of fabric, 2.8m (9ft) wide should be enough
to make a tablecloth and six matching serviettes.
Capsicum (p. 48) sells fabric in widths of 1.1m (3ft 6in)
or 2.5m (8ft 1in). The silks at McLennans (see above)
are 1–1.15m (3ft 3in–3ft 9in) wide. So you need around
0.5m (1ft 8in) to make a cushion cover.

Antiques
and ceramics

All the collectors are familiar with Nieuwe Spiegelstraat, where you'll find Amsterdam's finest antiques shops. Alongside the more prestigious dealers there are also less well-known places where real bargains can be found, particularly fine pieces of old and new Delftware, which you could never find elsewhere. Engraved or sculpted glass is also a popular part of the decor of traditional Dutch interiors.

Hogendoorn & Kaufman

Rokin, 124
☎ 638 27 36
Mon.-Sat. 10am-6pm,
Sun. noon-6pm.

The best place in town to buy modern Delft or Makkum ware. Pieces are selected in the two royal factories and are hand-decorated by the best craftsmen. Everything from lovely 13 x 13cm (5 x 5in) Delft tiles to elegant tulip vases, but you have to be prepared to spend some money – €22.70 for a decorated tile, from €265 for a tulip vase. The shop can arrange international delivery of anything you buy.

Holland Gallery De Munt

Muntplein, 12
☎ 623 22 71
Mon.-Sat. 10am-6pm.

Don't mistake this for a souvenir shop, in fact it specializes in Dutch china-ware. It sells only signed pieces produced by royal manufacturers such as Porceleyne Fles in Delft and Tichelaar in Makkum. China tiles from €25. Considerable choice.

Eduard Kramer

Nieuwe Spiegelstraat, 64
☎ 623 08 32
Mon.-Sat. 10am-6pm,
Sun. noon-6pm.

You have to pick you way with cat-like caution between the unbelievable piles of ceramics and porcelain in this antiques shop specializing in old Delft and Makkum pieces. Here you'll find the widest choice of glazed tiles – a little expensive if you want a complete makeover for your kitchen or bathroom,

but there's nothing to stop you using one as a coaster.

Kunstzalen A. Vecht

Nieuwe Spiegelstraat, 40
☎ 623 47 48
www.artonline.nl/vecht
Tue.-Sat. noon-6pm.

In the 18th century it was common to present people with an engraved glass as a souvenir of a family party, whether a religious occasion or simply for fun. These glasses, nowadays fairly rare, are decorated with coats of arms, maxims, people or landscapes. You will find some at this antiques shop, among other exceptional Venetian and German glasses.

Steensma & Van der Plas

Prinsengracht, 272
☎ 627 21 97 / 06 54 77 55 99
www.steensma.nl
Fri.-Sat. 11am-6pm, or by appointment

These items of office and shop furniture and accessories, designed between 1880 and 1920, are beautiful, simple and functional. A display of exceptional pieces, from large clocks to cabinets with sliding backs, in an attractive setting. Worth taking a look.

Toebosch

Nieuwe Spiegelstraat, 33-35

☎ 625 27 32
Mon.-Fri. 11am-5.30pm, Sat. 11am-5pm.

Amid the ticking of magnificent Dutch clocks, look out for the complicated feats of craftsmanship in the form of 18th-century music boxes, in all sizes from tiny to real displays of a cabinet-maker's skill. Sideboards, tables and chairs create a thoroughly Dutch interior.

Frides Laméris

Nieuwe Spiegelstraat, 55
☎ 626 40 66
Mon. 1-6pm, Tue. 10am-6pm,
Sat. 10am-5pm.

A specialist in antique ceramics and glassware from the 16th, 17th, and 18th centuries. You will find the kind of drinking horns and stemmed glasses ornamented with china often depicted in Dutch still-life paintings. There is also Delftware and Chinese porcelain.

Ingeborg Ravestijn

Nieuwe Spiegelstraat, 57
☎ 625 77 20
Mon.-Sat. 1-5pm (better to telephone in advance).

The stock in this general antiques shop includes lots of silverware and barbotine pottery. To add an original touch to your table, you can buy replicas of Dutch glasses

made in the Czech Republic. Prices depend on size, with the small glasses at around €22 and the largest (the tall flutes) €62.

H. C. van Vliet

Nieuwe Spiegelstraat, 74
☎ 622 77 82
Every day 10am-6pm and by appointment (better to telephone in advance).

Continuing the tradition of Dutch master glassworkers, this antiques shop is home to an extraordinary collection of 16th- and 17th-century European glass. The selection of engraved glasses is particularly fine. These delicate objects were originally given as gifts to mark a special occasion such as a christening, wedding or birthday. There are many beautiful pieces of Italian or Flemish origin, as well as a large collection of period Dutch ceramics.

SOTHEBY'S

To get an idea of antiques prices, take a look round Sotheby's. This famous British firm of auctioneers also has a branch in Amsterdam. Here you'll find sales catalogs showing the prices various items reached at auction. If you want to attend any of the sales, all the items are put on display beforehand.

De Boelelaan, 30 – Tram 4 (RAI Station)
☎ 550 22 00 – Mon.-Fri. 9am-5pm.

Bric-a-brac

Bric-a-brac is something of a tradition and is sold in all the city's markets. The real bargains are to be found in the antiques shops, where prices may be a bit dearer but there's less doubt about authenticity. However, wherever you choose to shop, treasures are there to be unearthed, and for anyone mad about china, the Queen's Day bonanza is not to be missed (see p. 33)!

Fifties-Sixties

Reestraat, 5
☎ 623 26 53
Tue.-Sat. 1-6pm.

You'll find the owner of this shop, who personally guarantees the authenticity of her stock, surrounded by a charming jumble of lighting equipment and household electrical goods from the 1930s to the 1960s. A fine selection of kitchen gadgets, crockery and lamps in absolutely unrepeatable designs, and they are not too expensive either. Not all of it would look right in every home, but fans of 1960s retro will be in seventh heaven. Expect to pay around €125 for a Philips lamp and €1,940 for a 1950s toaster.

& Klevering

Bloemgracht, 175-177
☎ 422 03 97
Tue.-Fri. 11am-6pm.

A large warehouse selling period furniture and antiques such as cast-iron enameled baths and 1930s double washbasins in marble or stone. For the country kitchen look, they also stock simple cupboards in white leaded or polished wood, perfect for storing your crockery.

De Weldaad

Reestraat, 1
☎ 627 00 77
Wed.-Sat. 11am-5pm.

Mirjam Verheyke raids 17th-century Amsterdam houses that have been marked for demolition to recover Delft tiles, blue-stone sinks, marble fireplaces, wooden shutters, cast-iron grilles, ornamentation from their façades, and other such items. Rummage through her other finds: stoneware *jenever* bottles, ceramics and glasses,

...s well as curios such as mounted exotic fish and shells. She is delighted to share her passion with her customers and her prices are considerably lower than those of the antiques dealers.

Tut-Tut

**Elandsgracht, 109
De Looier antiekmarkt)
☎ 627 79 60
Thu.-Sun. 11am-5pm.**

Among the antiques dealers in this little market is the stall specializing in old toys – dolls, robots, mechanical toys and Fleischmann, Dinky and Matchbox trains (sometimes in the original box). Be prepared to haggle!

Conny Mol

**Elandsgracht, 65
☎ 618 06 69
Sat. 11am-5pm or by appointment on
☎ 06 51 14 16 80.**

Conny Mol specializes in furniture, lighting and objects dating from 1850 to 1945. In the large range, you'll find lovely art-deco pieces such as lamps and wall-lights in glass and chrome. Mirrors with wrought iron frames are also big news here.

Meulendijks & Schuil

**Nieuwe Spiegelstraat, 45A
☎ 620 03 00
Mon.-Sat. 10am-6pm.**

An address to remember for all sailing fanatics and people interested in the history of the science of navigation, with old compasses, 18th-century sextants and chronometers. Loads of decorative and gift ideas, often less expensive than you'd expect.

Odds & Sods

**1e Looiersdwarsstraat, 11
☎ 616 84 40
Tue.-Sun.1-6pm.**

This boutique specializing in

the 1900s–30s contains entire sitting and dining rooms, as well as chandeliers, art-deco glasswork, pewter, glass and unusual objects such as collar boxes. A real treasure trove.

Silverplate

**Nes, 89
☎ 624 83 39
Tue.-Fri. noon-6pm,
Sat. 11am-5pm,
Sun. 1-5pm.**

A stone's thrown from Rokin, Kyra ten Kate has opened a shop selling reasonably priced 19th-century silverware and pieces in silver plate for a really elegant dinner table. A wide choice of both cutlery and dinner services items.

Nic Nic

**Gasthuismolensteeg, 5
☎ 622 85 23
Mon.-Fri. noon-6pm,
Sat. 10am-5pm.**

The owner of this shop is clearly doing just what she enjoys. The result is a stunning array of ironic bric-a-brac at reasonable prices: ceramics, figures of patron saints, 1960s and 1970s lighting, and candlesticks by Scandinavian designers for around €8.

Tobacco
and spirits

The song that begins "In the port of Amsterdam ..." evokes alcoholic
hazes and pipe smoke so, as you would expect, there are a large number
of stores dedicated to these products. In this port city, the former hub of a
vast colonial empire, there are also spice sellers whose scented wares
conjure vistas of Indonesia, the Molucca and the Celebes Islands.

P.G.C. Hajenius

Rokin, 92-96
Between the Dam and
Muntplein
☎ 623 74 94
Tue.-Sat. 9.30am-6pm (9pm
Thu.), Sun.-Mon. noon-6pm.

Even nonsmokers should visit
this smoker's paradise, where
the superb art-deco interior
has remained unchanged
since 1914. As soon as you step
through the door, you are
assailed by the mingled scents
of tobacco. With its period
wood paneling and shelves
filled with cigars, pipes and
tobacco jars, Hajenius is a
chic and classy shop with a
touch of old-fashioned
stuffiness that's rather
amusing, and has been
renowned for 170 years for
the subtle mix of flavors in
its cigars, from cigarillos to
coronas. You can also buy
every kind of luxury accessory
for smokers – lighters, boxes,
humidifiers, cigar cases and
a colossal choice of
earthenware, wooden and
meerschaum pipes.

Herboristerie
Jacob Hooy & Co

Kloveniersburgwal, 12
☎ 624 30 41
Mon. 1-6pm, Tue.-Fri.
10am-6pm, Sat. 10am-5pm

It's now the fifth generation
of Oldenbooms who stand
behind the antique counter of

his shop, which has been in heir family for a hundred and ifty years. They specialize in nedicinal herbs and spices (with 600 varieties), natural cosmetic products and candy, ncluding their famous iquorice drops. Even if you lecide not to buy anything, he shop itself is worth a visit ust to see the shelves lined with jars.

The Natural Health Company De Munt

Vijzelstraat, 1
☎ 624 45 33
Mon.-Fri. 9.30am-6.30pm (9pm Thu.), Sat. 9.30am-6.30pm, Sun. noon-6pm.

Vitamins and essential oils line he shelves of this small shop, while bubble bath with plant extracts, or unusual soaps scented with cinnabar, orange or even cannabis, are sure to iven up bath time! All the products are completely natural, for good health and a baby-soft skin

De Bierkoning

Paleisstraat, 125
☎ 625 23 36
Mon. 1-7pm, Tue.-Fri. 11am-7pm (9pm Thu.), Sat. 11am-6pm, Sun. 1-5pm.

However short your stay in Amsterdam, don't let it pass

without visiting a brasserie or other beer-drinking establishment. Beer has been flowing in Amsterdam's cafés since the 16th century. In De Bierkoning you'll find a selection of 850 different kinds of beer to take away. And for purists, there's even an appropriate glass to go with each type.

Van Coeverden

Leidsestraat, 58
☎ 624 51 50
Mon.-Sat. 9.30am-6pm, 7pm Wed. in winter, 8pm in summer.

A real, old-fashioned tobacco shop, with its tiled floor and dark furnishings displaying rows of pipes, cigar boxes,

packets of cigarettes and rolling tobacco. The walls themselves seem impregnated with the scent of the tobacco. Nothing seems to have changed here for decades and, even if you're not a smoker, step in to take a look at one of

Amsterdam's most typically traditional shops.

Oud Amsterdam

Nieuwendijk, 75
☎ 624 45 81
Mon.-Sat. 10am-6pm.

In this very busy shopping street, Oud Amsterdam ("Old Amsterdam") is an old-fashioned shop boasting beams decorated with small bottles of spirits. Behind the counter, with its patina of age, you can see the 50 or so Dutch liqueurs on display and particularly the 17 types of *jenever* distilled here and aged for between one and 17 years. Tasting essential.

A. van Wees distilleerderij de Ooievaar

Driehoekstraat, 7-10
☎ 626 77 52
www.de-ooievaar.nl
Mon.-Fri. 10am-5pm.

In this small corner of Jordaan, the coat of arms depicting home distillers decorates the baroque façade of a house where the Van Wees family have been distilling 16 sorts of *jenever* and 60 liqueurs since 1750. Rather than visiting the distillery, you could perhaps be party to the negotiations of *proeflokalen* retailers in the tasting room (no. 10) and, no doubt, snap up some amber liquid preserved in the superb stoneware bottles for your own consumption.

JENEVER OR BRANDY?

Jenever is flavored with herbs and can be drunk young or old. It can also be distilled with lemon or redcurrants. Many people also enjoy the fruit brandies, such as the Rose sans épines (Rose without Thorns), made by monks, or Oranje Bitter, a syrupy orange liqueur which is drunk on April 30, the Queen's birthday.

Coffee, tea
chocolate and spices

Would you like an *Amsterdammertje* or a *speculaas* with your coffee? If you don't want to look silly when faced with this kind of question, be sure to make an early visit to one of Amsterdam's excellent confectioners to sample the subtle flavors of bitter chocolate and ginger cakes. Then savor the aroma of freshly ground coffee emanating from one of the old cafés, most of which were founded at the time of the East India Company's first expeditions to the spice islands of the Far East. And if you'd like to try your hand at some Indonesian cooking, south Amsterdam is the place to go for the greatest range of exotic ingredients.

Geels & Co

Warmoesstraat, 67
☎ 624 06 83
Mon.-Sat. 9.30am-6pm.
Founded 140 years ago, this family business in the heart of the red-light district grinds 20 different types of coffee at the back of the shop.

De Plantage

Utrechtsestraat, 130
☎ 626 46 84
Mon. 1-6pm, Tue.-Fri. 10am-6pm, Sat. 10am-5.30pm.
Try to visit on a Thursday, when you will see 30 types of delicately flavored coffee being ground by hand. This is also the only place in town where you can try the teas and coffees before buying them! High tea is available on week-days, but you must book in advance.

Simon Lévelt

Prinsengracht, 180
☎ 624 08 23
Mon.-Fri. 10am-6pm, Sat. 10am-5pm.

Since 1839, this lovely store, decorated with wrought iron and situated opposite the Westerkerk, has been selling 25 different sorts of coffee, all ground on the premises, and 100 special blends of tea. A real institution.

Wijs & Zonen

Warmoesstraat, 102
☎ 624 04 36
Mon.-Sat. 10am-6pm.

A pretty little shop where the coffee is stored in enamel jars, giving off a wonderful aroma. Generations have watched the repetition of the same ritual, when a taster comes to verify the standard of the 40 different subtle blends of tea

Puccini Bomboni

Staalstraat, 17
☎ 626 54 74
Mon. noon-6pm, Tue.-Sat. 9am-6pm, Sun. noon-5pm.

In this beautiful shop, where the light filters through stained-glass windows, exquisite chocolates are piled on the counter in precarious pyramids. Made by Ans van Soelen to old-fashioned recipes using butter and cocoa and no preservatives, they are truly delicious but certainly not for weight watchers!

Toko Ramee

Ferdinand Bolstraat, 74
☎ 662 20 25
Tue.-Fri. 10am-7pm, Sat. 10am-6pm.

Krupuk, ayam, sambal, gado gado, bami, nasi — you could play a guessing game, trying to match these Indonesian names to what they are. On the other hand, if you want to buy with confidence, you'd be better off

asking the advice of the charming Moluccan lady who sells the spices and can also explain to you how to use them to best advantage in your cooking. You can bring a real hint of adventure to your meals by concocting some true Indonesian dishes, and you can, of course, use these ingredients very successfully to spice up Western-style food.

Arnold Cornélis

Elandsgracht, 78
☎ 625 85 85
Van Baerlestraat, 93
☎ 662 12 28
Mon.-Fri. 8.30am-6pm, Sat. 8.30am-5pm.

In this renowned patisserie you'll find not only delicious fruit tarts (*limburgse vlaai*), but also candy, butter biscuits, *speculaas* — delicious with coffee — marzipan and chocolate, all homemade.

Australian Homemade

Leidsestraat, 101
☎ 622 08 97

Every day 11am-11pm (8pm Sat.).

Chocoholics and art-lovers alike will melt at the sight of these

chocolates, all decorated with aboriginal designs. The picture of a kangaroo tells you it's a tea-flavored center, while tortoises

indicate almond centers and the fish are ginger-flavored. Come and discover the other flavors for yourself, and don't miss the freshly made ice cream.

Unlimited Delicious

Haarlemmerstraat, 122
☎ 622 48 29
www.unlimiteddelicious.nl
Mon.-Sat. 9am-6pm, Sun. noon-6pm.

There's nothing dull about these chocolates — white, dark or milk, the flavor of cocoa beans is subtly enhanced by balsamic vinegar, Espelette peppers, red peppers and even tomatoes! There are some 25 different combinations, each one unusual and unique. Reserve a month in advance and you can even learn how to make them for yourself, under the instruction of a master chocolate-maker.

THE JOURNEY OF THE COFFEE PLANT

The word "coffee" comes from the name Kaffa, a region in Ethiopia where the coffee tree originates. When Arab merchants introduced the drink to Yemen, it became known as Arabica or Moka, the name of the port from which it was mostly exported. In 1714, Pancras, the Mayor of Amsterdam, gave King Louis XIV of France a few coffee plants which the Dutch had acclimatized in their Indonesian colony of Batavia. The French then introduced them to Guyana and Brazil.

Secondhand

The Dutch love a bargain. For secondhand clothes, try the markets on Waterlooplein, Noordemarkt and Nieuwmarkt, where the great revival of 1970s clothing is in full swing. If you prefer more of a classic look, it's better to go to the specialist shops in Jordaan. Many shops in Kalverstraat and Nieuwendijk have sales on all year round, and, like everywhere else, the smartest time to buy is when you see posters in the windows proclaiming "Uitverkoop" and "Opruiming." Sales are held twice a year, starting in the last week of December and June and continuing for about a month.

Jo-Jo Outfitters and Jo-Jo Shop

Huidenstraat, 23
☎ 623 34 76
Mon. noon–6pm,
Tue.–Sat. 11am–6pm,
Sun. 2pm–6pm.

British and American unlabeled brands for men, which are however, clearly recognizable as designer wear. Quality and durability are the watchwords, with shirts, trousers and jackets from €68 up to €181.50 for the best stuff. Nothing very imaginative, but they're all good quality items.

Lady Day

Hartenstraat, 9
☎ 623 58 20

Mon.–Sat. 11am–6pm (9pm Thu.), Sun. 1–6pm.

Anyone with a penchant for retro clothing will be in

heaven here. Most of the stock is vintage Americana from the 50s, 60s and 70s, and with evening dresses, suits, children's outfits and fashion accessories, you can kit out the whole family under one roof. Expect to pay around €19 for a shirt, €35 for a pair of trousers, €35 to €125 for an evening dress and a maximum of €89 for a leather coat.

Callas 43

Haarlemmerdijk, 43
☎ 427 37 90
Mon.–Sat. noon–6pm.

Luxury secondhand gear, with clothing, jewelry and accessories by Karl Lagerfeld,

YSL, Dior, Edgar Vos and other prestige brands for a third of the normal price. A very popular shop where you can find real bargains. Some think this alone justifies their trip. An address to keep under your hat.

Marché aux puces

**Westerstraat
and Noordermarkt
Mon. 9am-1pm.**

If you like rummaging around for a bargain, you'll be in your element here. All along Westerstraat, you'll find stalls selling secondhand goods, such as fabrics, kitchenware and clothing. There's also a small flea market on Noordermarkt, where you can take your pick from Dutch chandeliers at bargain prices, wooden ice skates and heaps of fun knick-knacks.

John's Fiets Inn

**Nieuwe Kerkstraat, 84
☎ 623 06 66
Tue.-Fri. 9am-5pm,
Sat. 11am-4pm.**

Sugar pink, leopard skin, with a child seat or a basket to carry your dog – however you like your bicycle, this is the place to find a bargain. Dutch makes of bicycle Gazelle, Union and Burco are nearly half price, so

prices for a good machine start at €140 and you will find an excellent one for €200 to €300. Surprisingly, ladies' bicycles are more expensive. You can be sure that you are buying a genuine, solid bicycle with a back-pedal brake that is made in Holland.

Laura Dols en de Verkleed Komeet

**Wolvenstraat, 7
☎ 624 90 66
Mon.-Sat. 11am-6pm,
Sun. 1-6pm.**

Here fans of 1940s and 1950s nostalgia will find everything they could wish for to dress themselves from head to toe. From beautiful satin slips to a hat with a veil and matching gloves and handbag, there's an amazingly wide choice at unbelievably low prices (crocodile-skin handbag from

€14, hat from €12). There's also loads of wonderful gift ideas, such as beauty essentials in a kid-leather case, glittering costume jewelry and horn-rimmed sunglasses.

Second Best

**Wolvenstraat, 18
☎ 422 02 74
Mon. 1-6pm, Tue.-Fri.
11am-6pm, Sat. 11am-6pm.**

Armani, Ted Lapidus, Versace and Sine qua non suits at a quarter of their price new! Very wide choice of trousers from €10 to €70.

Second Line

**Herengracht, 404
Wed.-Sat. 11am-6pm.**

The same principle as Second Best in this shop specializing in designer-name clothes ... for men.

Zipper

**Huidenstraat, 7
☎ 623 73 02
Mon.-Sat. 11am-6pm (9pm
Thu.), Sun. 1-5pm.**

A great selection of clothing for 20-30 year-olds at amazing prices, with slightly worn jeans, checked shirts, leather bomber jackets, little floral dresses and flares. At Zipper you can construct a total 1970s look for next to nothing. Of course, if you're over 40 you can re-purchase the outfits you used to wear as a teenager!

DE ZWAAN SALE-ROOM

You can buy absolutely anything from the city sale-room. The prices usually stay fairly low, so make sure you get some information about the date of the next sale before you arrive (some are held at the weekend). Items to be sold are put on display before the start of the auction, so you can examine a piece of furniture or other item that interests you at your leisure. Of course, it's better if you speak Dutch and don't put your hand up too rashly. To avoid surprises and make sure the item you want doesn't slip through your fingers, it's best to leave a bid with the auctioneer before the sale starts.

**Keizersgracht, 474 – ☎ 622 04 47
Mon.-Sun. 9am-5pm, Fri. 9am-4pm.**

Practicalities

Where to go

Whether you are a lover of early music or a crazy clubber, Amsterdam will fulfill all your expectations. Nightlife is concentrated in three districts, whatever the season. Leidseplein, full of restaurants, theatres, bars and jazz clubs, is the haunt of young, fairly well-behaved people. In the red-light district around the station, with its neon signs, women on display in shop windows, shady bars and countless sex shops, life goes on all night long,

FINDING YOUR WAY

Many bars and clubs now have websites where you can usually find detailed directions, any information on dress codes and facilities and often a map of how to get there.

attracting a crowd of voyeuristic tourists, dealers and customers. But the real heartbeat of the Amsterdam nightlife can be heard around Rembrandtplein. This is where you'll find the coolest bars, the weirdest clubs and the wildest people, where gay revelers rub shoulders with students, foreigners and Amsterdam's upper crust, who can be observed out slumming it with the rest. Here too, if you want, you can dance all night long to the deafening sound of techno and house music. As soon as the weather improves, the streets are filled with music and musical events, most of which can be enjoyed for free. There are open-air rock, pop and jazz concerts and brass bands, particularly in Vondelpark and Amsterdamse Bos. Classical music also takes to the streets, settling on the barges moored along the canalsides or invading Jordaan's small squares.

Cafés

Around 8pm the beer and spirits start to flow. Barriers between different sections of society come down in the cafés, where Amsterdammers prefer to spend their evenings out, and where they can sit every night until 1am and as late as 2 or 3am on Friday and Saturday nights. From the unpretentious local cafés, where the customers sometimes break into song, to the "brown cafés," where they drink strong beers with *jenever* chasers, to the cool cafés, where the young clubbers gather before going off to dance all night, the coffee-shops where people drop in for a quick puff of weed and the gay bars where leather gear is the rule, there's an enormous choice and you can easily move from one to another. They all stand side by side, and you'll get a warm welcome in all of them.

Amsterdam nightlife: the look

Don't bother with a classy wardrobe if you're going out in Amsterdam. The ambience is relaxed everywhere you go, and that goes for even the smartest, most formal places, such as the Muziektheather and the Concertgebouw. Older people might want to dress up for the occasion, but it's certainly not obligatory and you'll be allowed in without. You don't even have to wear a tie in the casino, although they do draw the line at shorts and trainers, and at the hippest clubs, the more original, unusual and cool you look, the more likely it is that the bouncer will let you in.

Nightclubs and jazz-bars

Nightclubs open their doors at 11pm, but don't expect to find many people there that early. Before going to their favorite clubs, Amsterdammers take a tour of the cafés, setting off to dance around 1am and generally staying on until closing time (4am on weeknights and 5am on Friday and Saturday nights). It will cost you between €4 and €15 for entry, depending on what day it is, and no-one gets any special treatment. The door price sometimes includes the cost of a membership card, which enables you to go again another night. Bands are normally playing in the jazz clubs and music cafés by around 9pm. You can get in for nothing as long as you buy drinks. Take a look at www.good2b.nl, www.

underwateramsterdam.com and www.urbanguide.nl to discover the hippest places to be.

Concerts

All year round there are concerts of every kind, from rock, pop and world music to classical and chamber music, as well as theatre, dance, opera and cabaret in a huge variety of places, from the ordinary to the magnificent. To plan the evening to suit you among the hundreds of events on offer

each week, there are two monthly magazines distributed in cafés, hotels and tourist offices. *Amsterdam Day by Day* is in English (€1.75) and has daily listings, while free mag *Uitkrant*, published by the AUB (Amsterdams Uit Buro) in Dutch, provides a complete calendar of cultural events. There's a free supplement called *Pop & Jazz Uitlijst* that comes out twice a week and

gives you information on rock, blues and jazz concerts and what's on in the clubs. Another magazine worth looking out for is the *Amsterdam Weekly*.

Reserving tickets

Although the most prestigious early music concerts, operas and ballets are usually sold out weeks in advance, it's often possible to get tickets the day before, or on the night itself, though you shouldn't expect to get a very good seat. Unless it's a last-minute decision, don't go to the concert hall or theater to reserve your seats. The central booking office of the AUB Leidseplein, 26, near the Stadschouwburg, is open Monday to Saturday 10am-6pm and until 9pm on Thursday, and noon to 6pm on Sunday. The €2 commission is also charged by the booking offices in the venues themselves and all credit cards are accepted. Remember that pre-booking for the same evening closes at 4pm. After that you have to go to the venue itself, where tickets are sold until an hour before the event starts. Seats that have been booked and paid for will be resold if not collected an hour before the curtain rises.

RESERVING TICKETS BY PHONE/ONLINE

If you have a credit card, you can make a theatre or concert booking from your hotel by calling the Uitlijn, or by visiting the website www.uitlijn.nl (commission of €2.50 per ticket), or by calling ☎ 0 900 0191 0191 (€0.40 per minute) every day, 9am-9pm (€3 per ticket commission). The VVV offices also handle bookings, but you have to go there in person (Leidseplein, 106 or Stationsplein, 10).

Classical

1 - Muziektheater
2 - Bourse de Berlage
3 - Concertgebouw
4 - Bourse de Berlage

Music – Dance Theater

Concertgebouw

Concertgebouwplein, 2-6
☎ 573 05 73
Reservations every day
10am-5pm on ☎ 671 83 45
www.concertgebouw.nl
Seat prices: €15 to €35.

This hall, renowned for the quality of its acoustics, is the home of the Royal Orchestra of the Netherlands, conducted by Mariss Janssons. This temple to classical music stages concerts by the greatest early music ensembles, especially those playing baroque music.

Bourse de Berlage

Damrak, 243
☎ 521 75 75
www.berlage.com
kassa@orkest.nl
Reservations: Tue.-Fri.
2-5pm, or 2 hours before
the concert
Seat prices: €10 to €12.50.

This is the home of the Philharmonic Orchestra of the Netherlands, as well as the National Orchestra of Chamber Music, which in fact from now on will play more at the Concertgebouw (www.orkest.nl). It has also recently become the permanent home of the newly formed Amsterdam Symphony Orchestra, consisting of 70 musicians conducted by Peter Sánta, who play in the famous 1,200-seat Grote Zaal.

Muziektheater

Amstel, 3
☎ 551 89 11
www.muziektheater.nl
Reservations on ☎ 625 54 55
Seat prices: dance €12.50
to €30, opera €25 to €70.
Concerts: 7.30pm, 8pm,
8.15pm; Sun. 1.30pm
or 2pm.

The "Stopera" complex, which opened in 1988, seats up to 1,600 spectators. The national ballet and the Netherlands opera are based here and stage fairly eclectic programs ranging from classical works to new productions.

Stadsschouwburg

Leidseplein, 26
☎ **523 77 00**
www.ssba.nl
Reservations Mon.-Sat.
10am-6pm on ☎ 624 23 11
Seat prices: €11 to €35.
Stages plays, concerts and contemporary dance performances by companies from the Netherlands and other countries.

Koninklijk Theater carré

Amstel, 115-125
☎ **622 52 25**
www.theatercarre.nl
Reservations every day 9am-9pm on ☎ 0 900 25 25 255
Performances at 8pm; circus at noon, 3pm, 4pm, 8pm.
Seat prices: €14 to €98.

This former circus hall has been a venue since 1887 for grand spectaculars of all kinds, including circuses and a variety of musical shows.

Nieuwe de la Mar Theater

Marnixstraat, 404
☎ **530 53 02**
www.nieuwedelamar.nl
Seat prices: €15 to €25
Performances at 3pm and 8.15pm.

This theater specializes in cabaret and popular music and dance from all around the world.

BUT ALSO…

You can also listen to classical music in Vondelpark, in the English and Walloon churches in the Beguinage and in the Van Loon museum.

Muziektheater

De Ijsbreker

Weesperzijde, 23
☎ **693 90 93**
Reservations Mon.-Fri.
1-5pm.
This hall by the Amstel is the home of contemporary music (John Cage, Maurício Kagel, Salvatore Sciarrino, Georg Katzer), with concerts of accordion and electronic music as well as various experimental groups.

KIT Tropentheater

Linnaeusstraat, 2
☎ **568 85 00**
www.tropentheater.nl
Reservations Mon.-Sat.
noon-6pm
Seat prices: €17.50.
Attached to the Tropical Museum, this theatre might be small but nevertheless qualifies as a podium for non-Western cultures. Troubadours from the Moroccan South, Arab classical music, Indian music, Asian theatre and dance plus much more appear on the program.

Felix Meritis

Keizersgracht, 324
☎ **623 13 11**
www.felix.meritis.nl
Performances at 8pm.

English-language avant-garde plays, as well as modern dance productions and jazz and classical music concerts, are all staged in the prestigious setting of this theatre, which first opened in 1787.

Nieuwe Kerk

Dam
☎ **638 69 09**
www.nieuwekerk.nl
Entrance: Sun. €6, Thu. €3.

Every Sunday evening at 8pm and Thursday at 12.30pm, from June to the end of August, there is a concert of organ music in the grand setting of the New Church. The recitals include music by Bach, Purcell and Buxtehude.

Casino

Holland Casino Amsterdam

Max Euweplein, 62
☎ **521 11 11**
Every day 1.30pm-3am
Entrance charge: €3.50.

If you're tempted by the roulette wheel, black jack or poker, why not try the new casino near Leidseplein? The building is nothing special but the fever which grips the gamblers is the same as in older casinos. The café-restaurant on the lower floor has a lovely waterside terrace and stages cabaret shows from Wednesday to Sunday, starting at 6.30pm. You can also waltz to the sound of the orchestra.

Bars and clubs

1 - Museum
2 - Café Cox
3 - Dulac

Proeflokalen or "tasting houses," formerly attached to distilleries, offer a wide variety of *jenevers*, *korewijn*, and other spirits, as well as beers and whiskies. "Brown cafés," with their nicotine-stained walls, and "white cafés," with their designer decor, are the places to be from 5pm. They are busiest on Friday and Saturday evening when the music is on loud and the beer flows fast.

Proeflokalen

De Admiraal

Herengracht, 319
☎ 645 43 34
Mon.-Sat. 4.30-11pm.

With barrels piled up to the ceiling and wooden tables where you can enjoy the Van Wees *jenevers*, this

is the oldest distillery in Jordaan. You can also enjoy a candle-lit dinner in this rustic setting.

De Ooievaar

Sint Olofspoort, 1
(corner of Zeedijk)
☎ 420 80 04
Mon.-Fri. 3pm-1am,
Sat.-Sun. 1pm-1am.

The impression that this *proeflokaal* appears to be on a slight tilt is not because you have drunk too many little frosted glasses of perfumed *oud*, but rather that it is extremely old, dating from 1620. Literally named "The Stalk," it is one of the oldest and most pleasant bars of its kind.

Wynand Fockink

Pijlsteeg, 31
☎ 639 26 95
Every day 3-9pm.

In a small street behind the Dam, this former distillery, founded in 1679, has reopened as a cozy bar where you can sample local products and other brands of liqueurs, as well as *jenever* flavored with coriander, aniseed and herbs.

In de Wildeman

Kolsteeg, 3
☎ 638 23 48
Mon.-Sat. noon-1am.

Near the station and red-light district, this attractive bar with its copper chandeliers, wood paneling and black and white tiling evokes an intimate scene by one of the Dutch old masters. You will find a choice of 150 kinds of beer, including 18 on tap.

De Still

Spuistraat, 326A
☎ 427 68 09
www.destill.nl
Mon.-Thu. 5pm-1am, Fri.-Sat 3pm-3am, Sun. 3pm-1am.

Still means "tranquility" in Dutch, and it is important to take a bit of time out to appreciate the bouquet and aromas of some of the 300 different types of whiskey which is the specialty of this bar. There are famous malts such as Macallen, Glenfiddich and Highland Park, but also less known ones such as Old Pulteney and Islay, distilled on the tiny Scottish island of Caol Ila. Live jazz on the third Thursday of the month.

"Brown" cafés, "white" cafés

Café Chris

Bloemstraat, 42
☎ 624 59 42
Mon.-Thu. 3pm-1am, Fri.-Sat. 3pm-2am, Sun. 3pm-9pm.

This old "brown" café (dating to 1642) in Jordaan, near Westerkerk, is very popular among students.

De Druif

Rapenburgerplein, 83
☎ 624 45 30
Every day 11am-1am.

Well away from the main tourist areas, on the old docks, you will find this genuinely traditional café in a former *jenever* distillery.

De Twee Zwaantjes

Prinsengracht, 114
☎ 625 27 29
www.detweezwaantjes.nl
Fri. 6pm-3am, Sat. 3pm-3am, Sun. 3pm-1am.

A typical Jordaan "brown" café and former meeting-place for local brewers and workmen. Live music at weekends from 10pm or whenever the customers break into song. A mixed crowd and very "Jordaan" atmosphere – in other words, down-to-earth and fun.

Museum

Linnaeustraat, 29
☎ 665 09 56
Mon.-Thu. noon-1am, Fri.-Sat. noon-1am, Sun. 3pm-1am.

Near the Tropenmuseum, a fantastic café-restaurant opened by Cor Hameleers, a musician-artist and fans of Brittany. Good daily specials (from €10.50 to €15) served from 6.30pm and a friendly atmosphere.

De Engelbewaarder

KloFriiersburgwal, 57
☎ 625 37 72
Every day noon-1am (3am weekends).

There's a very relaxed atmosphere in this friendly café, which is the haunt of many newspaper people. Sunday is jazz day, when jazz-lovers come to enjoy the afternoon jam sessions.

BUT ALSO…

As you make your way around the city, try and call in at **De Drie Fleschjes**, the best place to enjoy a *borrel* of *jenever* (p. 43); sample the unbeatable choice of *jenevers* and spirits at **In de Olofspoort** (p. 51); try barrel-aged *korewijn* in **Hooghoudt** (p. 59).

PAYING THE CHECK

If you sit out on the terrace, you must settle the check immediately. Inside "brown cafés" the waiter will note what you drink as you go along in his notebook. Be warned that those little shots of *jenever* can often add up to a nasty surprise when the time comes to pay.

Dulac

Haarlemmerstraat, 118
☎ 624 42 65
Every day noon-1am (3am Fri.-Sat.).

A large, smart café near the central station, decorated in a skillful blend of art deco and neo-gothic, with live jazz groups on a Saturday night and Sunday afternoon.

Mulligan's

Amstel, 100
☎ 622 13 30
Mon.-Thu. 4pm-1am, Fri.-Sat. 2pm-3am, Sun. 2pm-1am.

A hot, alcohol-fumed atmosphere in this Irish pub with live folk groups playing Celtic music at the weekends. Popular with the Irish, of course.

Café Cox

Marnixstraat, 429
☎ 620 72 22
Every day 5pm-1am (3am Fri.-Sat.).

Favorite haunt of actors and directors from the Stadschouwburg next door. The kitchen is open until half-past midnight.

De Balie

Kleine Gartmanplantsoen, 10
☎ 553 51 30
Every day 10am-1am (2am Fri.-Sat.).

This large café, located near Leidseplein, is the locals' favorite stop after a visit to the cinema or theater or before a night in a club. Snacks and light meals until 1am.

Van Puffelen

Prinsengracht, 375
☎ **624 62 70**
Mon.-Fri. 3-11pm,
Sat.-Sun. noon-11pm.

Cozy atmosphere, candlelight and, if you're so inclined, light meals with an Italian and French bias.

Pop, rock, blues & jazz clubs

Alto Jazz Café

Korte Leidsedwarsstraat, 115 (Leidseplein)
☎ **626 32 49**
Every day 9pm-2am (4am weekends).

Different types of band play live here, with a lively jam session on Wednesdays with Hans Dulfer, a pillar of the Amsterdam jazz scene. Hein van der Haag plays piano on Mondays.

Bimhuis

Oudeschans, 73-77
☎ **623 13 61**
www.bimhuis.nl
Concerts Thu.-Sat.
(€12–€18)
Closed Jul.-Aug.

BUT ALSO…

On your wanders: **Hoppe**, one of the oldest "brown cafés" on the Spui (p. 40); **'t Smalle** Smalle in Jordaan, established in 1780 (p. 57); **'t Papenei-land** tiled in old Delft (p.57); the trendy **Café Welling** (p. 65); the wood-paneling and priceless bottles in the old wooden house **In 't Aepjen** (p. 69); the terrace along the Amstel and the fashion-able clientele of the **Café De Jaren** (p. 45).

A temple to jazz, where great international jazz musicians come to play. Jam sessions on Mondays, Tuesdays and Fridays.

Cruise Inn

Zuiderzeeweg, 29
Bus 37 until Amstelstation
☎ **692 71 88**
www.cruise-inn.com
Sat. 9pm-1am (3am for concerts).

Fans of good ol' 50s rock-n-roll gather at this club in the Schellingwoude district every Saturday night for some very acrobatic dancing.

Paradiso

Weteringschans, 6-8
☎ **626 45 21**
www.paradiso.nl
Variable hours: inquire.

When it ceased to be used as a church, this old building became a hang-out for hippies, who came to sit in clouds of incense and marijuana smoke, listening to Indian music. Now it's a venue for all kinds of music, from modern classical works to Mexican Mariachis, electronic funk, jazz and salsa sounds. VIP nights on Fridays and paradiso on Saturdays for those who still want to come and dance.

Café Bourbon Street

Leidsekruisstraat, 6
☎ **623 34 40**
Every day 10pm-4am (5am Fri.-Sat.)
Entrance charge Sat. (€5).

A jazz club playing extremely loud music that is packed at weekends. Jam session every Monday at 10.30pm and blues, rock and funk bands all other nights from 10pm onwards.

't Geveltje

Bloemgracht, 170
☎ **623 99 83**

Every day 8pm-1am.

A small "brown café" right in the heart of Jordaan where jazz professionals have played for more than 25 years. Jam session on Monday and Friday at 9pm world music concert on Wednesday at 8pm.

De Badcuyp

1e Sweelinckstraat, 10
☎ **675 96 69**
www.badcuyp.nl
Every day except Mon.
6pm-1am (2am weekends).

An alternative café-theatre in the newly cool Albert Cuyp area where you can dance and listen to live music in the evening Latin or African jazz on Saturday jam sessions every Sunday, salsa on Wednesday, world music or Thursday, surprise guest on Friday. Light meals are available until 10pm.

Zuiderbad

Hobbemastraat, 26
☎ **679 22 17**
Concerts to 8pm
Entrance charge: €12.50.

One Saturday every month this attractive art-deco swimming pool provides the backdrop for a jazz concert organized by the pianist Polo de Haas. No reason why you shouldn't swim a few lengths while you're there as the sound is relayed under water as well!

Melkweg

Lijnbaansgracht, 234
☎ **531 81 81**
www.melkweg.nl
Variable hours; inquire.

It's a sign of the times – this former dairy near Leidseplein, once the capital of 1970s pop and a gathering place for hippies, has had a total makeover. Today, it's a venue for films, pop and world-music gigs, avant-garde theater

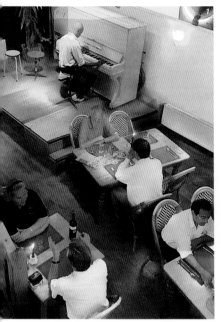

1 - De Badcuyp
2 - Les canaux la nuit
3 - De Admiraal

productions and even a restaurant. For the nostalgic, there's a disco at weekends, with DJs hosting theme nights.

Cocktail bars

Arc

Reguliersdwarsstraat, 44
☎ 689 70 70
www.bararc.com
Fri.-Sat. 11h-3am, Sun.-Thu. 4pm-1am

A fabulously glamorous venue where you can nibble on appetizing snacks while you mull over the fantastic list of cocktails, mixed by the shaker boys. On Fridays, the hyper-hot, hyper-gay crowd need no encouragement from the renowned DJs to hit the dance floor (9pm onwards). Special offers on Wednesday (cocktails cost €5 all evening) and happy hour from 5 to 7pm.

Bamboo Bar

Lange Leidsedwarsstraat, 66
☎ 624 39 93
Every day 9pm-3am, (4am Fri.-Sat.).

This tropically themed bar offers cocktails to blow your mind and good house and hip-hop music mixed by DJs.

Joia

Korte Leidsedwarsstraat, 45
☎ 626 67 69
Sun.-Wed. 6pm-1am, Thu. 6pm-2am, Fri. Sat. 6pm-3am.

Mirrors on the walls and ceiling, crimson velvet, subdued lighting …a mixture of a Parisian brothel circa 1930, an oriental salon and a jazz club – most unexpected in this touristy area. In essence a lounge bar, with excellent cocktails, including the Cosmopolitan, as mixed by Salvatore.

Odessa

Veemkade, 259
☎ 419 30 10
www.de-odessa.nl
Every day 4pm-1am (3am Fri.-Sat.).

The hippest bar in Amsterdam is on board a Ukrainian fishing boat moored behind the old IJhaven warehouses, 15 minutes' walk from the station. Groove and soul sessions with a DJ on Friday and Saturday from 10pm, barbecue on the bridge in summer on Sunday and unforgettable cocktails to ensure a pleasurable voyage.

Lime

Zeedijk, 104
☎ 639 30 20
Every day 5pm-1am (3am Fri.-Sat.).

Right in the heart of the Nieuwmarkt Chinatown, total

immersion in the golden oldies of the 1960s and 1970s as you enjoy vodka-based cocktails sunk into the super-soft armchairs. Good, cool music and a generally laid-back feel.

Cineac

Reguliersbreestraat, 31-33
☎ 530 68 88
**Sun.-Thu. 6pm-1am
(3am Fri.-Sat.).**

In the same street as the extravagant Tuschinski (p. 59), this cinema stands out by the sobriety of its functionalism-inspired façade (J. Duiker, 1934). Recently renovated at great expense, it is now a very select club where the rich and famous must see and be seen. The four levels of tables and armchairs, amid opulent red and silver decor, focus on an impressive bar, where champagne is served with caviar and sashimis. There is a strict dress code enforced at the door, and you can see why.

Suite

Sint Nicolasstraat, 43
☎ 489 65 31
**Sun.-Thu. 6pm-1am
(3am Fri.-Sat.).**

This ultra cozy lounge bar is the meeting place for beautiful people and a place to head for after dinner, when you can share a few tapas and have a drink while you enjoy the funk and rock'n'roll music.

Clubbing

Jimmy Woo

Korte Leidsedwarsstraat, 18
☎ 626 31 50
**www.jimmywoo.nl
Wed.-Thu. and Sun. 8pm-3am, Fri.-Sat. 8pm-4am.**
This attractive bar, decked out like a Hong Kong opium den, has an underground dance floor that is currently very much in

vogue. Excellent sound system pumping out urban music, from hip-hop to garage. No dress code but the people on the door are very selective if you're not on the guest list.

More

Rozengracht, 133
☎ 344 64 02
**www.expectmore.nl
Wed.-Sun. 10pm-4am
(5am Fri.-Sat.).**

On the ground floor is a big room hung with mirrors and net, where you eat reclining on beds. Arab jazz pumps up from the basement where you will find one of the trendiest night-clubs of the moment. There are theme evenings with excellent DJs — on Wednesday it's gay night, Thursday is deep house and techno, Friday is Latin, groove and funk; and Saturday, Club Risk.

Korsakoff

Lijnbaansgracht, 161
☎ 625 78 54
**www.korsakoff.nl
Sun.-Thu. 11pm-3am
(4am Fri.-Sat.).**

This is *the* night-spot for alternative clubbers (the children of the squatting movement) who get their kicks from punk rock, heavy metal and grunge while drinking the bar dry of relatively inexpensive beer. It is still free to get in!

Supperclub

Jonge Roelensteeg, 21
☎ 344 64 00
**www.supperclub.nl
Dinner: Sun.-Thu 7.30pm-1am (3am Fri.-Sat.).**

This is the place to be right now. For around €60 you can enjoy the sensual experience of dining while you recline barefoot on a bed. The surprises are plentiful — you may get a shiatsu massage, or perhaps it will be techno night.

Don't miss the fire-eating waiters carrying the plates. A restaurant reservation gives access to the Lounge club as well (reserved for members at the weekend).

Winston International

Warmoestraat, 129
☎ 623 13 80
**www.winston.nl
Fri.-Sun. midnight-4am,
Mon.-Thu. 8pm-3am.**

A different kind of music every night, with DJ Polack overseeing dizzy night on Fridays; DJ G. Bean offering Night Fever on Saturday, while on Sunday, it's Club Vegas. There is a different dress code depending on the theme and on Monday, the Big F is dedicated to a mixture of food (vegetarian) fashion, friends and fun.

Club Zyon

Nieuwezijds Voorburgwal, 161
**www.clubzyon.com
Sun.-Thu. 10pm-4am
(5am Fri.-Sat.).**

Two clubs in one. Zyon 1 has futuristic decor with a bar overhanging the dance floor and Zyon 2 is more of a lounge bar with canapés and a bar-lounge for VIPs. One of the best night-spots for dancing to house music, trance, techno, R&B and hip-hop mixed by DJs from all over the world. There's not much chance of getting in if you're over 30.

Club It

Amstelstraat, 24
☎ 625 01 11
**www.it.nl
Thu.-Sun. 11pm-4am
(5am Fri.-Sat.).**

The most extravagant of the Amsterdam nightclubs, where you need to leave any inhibitions behind as you step over the front door-step. House music, with a

1 - Panama
2 - Winston International
3 - Supperclub

hot and hip vibe enhanced by the revealing fancy dress that most people wear. You can go just to dance, however. Saturday is gay night.

Sinners in HeaFri

Wagenstraat, 3-7
www.sinners.nl
Every day 11pm-4am (5am Fri.-Sat.).

This small club tends to serve as a meeting place before people head off to dance at the other Rembrandtplein night-clubs. The decor is a strange combination of church and castle with house and techno music pumping out over three floors.

Panama

Oostelijke Handelskade, 4
☎ 311 86 86
www.panama.nl

Wed.-Thu. 6pm-3am, Fri.-Sat. 6pm-midnight.

This former industrial building in the new trendy area of the old IJhaven docks has become a multi-cultural hot-spot with a restaurant serving Mediterranean cuisine (open until 1.30am on Friday and Saturday), a tango studio, cocktail bar and nightclub, where Thursday through to Sunday are generally Latin and jazz nights.

Supperclub Cruise

☎ 344 64 03
www.suppercruise.nl
By arrangement.

On Friday and Saturday the Supperclub team take to the canals. You meet next to the boat moored behind the central station. Once on board, you have the choice of "La Salle Neige" where you can recline on an

immaculate bed, or "Le Bar Noir" where you can enjoy cocktails and dance to house and techno. An interesting experience, particularly on hot summer evenings (admittedly few and far between). Reservations needed.

Club Arena

's Gravesandestraat, 51
☎ 694 74 44
www.hotelarena.nl
Fri.-Sat. 10pm-3am.

A new nightclub that is very popular with the young crowd, housed in the fresco-decorated chapel of a former orphanage and dating from 1890. The two floors have very different vibes, with tunes from the 1960s and '70s on the first and third Saturday of the month, and a more '80s and '90s theme on the second and fourth Saturdays.

Metric Conversion Chart

Women's sizes

Blouses/dresses

U.K.	U.S.A.	EUROPE
8	6	36
10	8	38
12	10	40
14	12	42
16	14	44
18	16	46

Sweaters

U.K.	U.S.A.	EUROPE
8	6	44
10	8	46
12	10	48
14	12	50
16	14	52

Shoes

U.K.	U.S.A.	EUROPE
3	5	36
4	6	37
5	7	38
6	8	39
7	9	40
8	10	41

Men's sizes

Shirts

U.K.	U.S.A.	EUROPE
14	14	36
$14^{1}/_{2}$	$14^{1}/_{2}$	37
15	15	38
$15^{1}/_{2}$	$15^{1}/_{2}$	39
16	16	41
$16^{1}/_{2}$	$16^{1}/_{2}$	42
17	17	43
$17^{1}/_{2}$	$17^{1}/_{2}$	44
18	18	46

Suits

U.K.	U.S.A.	EUROPE
36	36	46
38	38	48
40	40	50
42	42	52
44	44	54
46	46	56

Shoes

U.K.	U.S.A.	EUROPE
6	8	39
7	9	40
8	10	41
9	10.5	42
10	11	43
11	12	44
12	13	45

More useful conversions

1 centimeter	0.39 inches	1 inch	2.54 centimeters
1 meter	1.09 yards	1 yard	0.91 meters
1 kilometer	0.62 miles	1 mile	1. 61 kilometers
1 liter	2.12 (US) pints	1 (US) pint	0.47 liters
1 gram	0.035 ounces	1 ounce	28.35 grams
1 kilogram	2.2 pounds	1 pound	0.45 kilograms

Published by AA Travel Publishing.

First published as Un grand week-end à Amsterdam: © Hachette Livre (Hachette Tourisme), 2005
Written by Katherine Vanderhaeghe and Alix Delalande
Maps within the book © Hachette Tourisme

Published by AA Publishing, a trading name of Automobile Association Developments Limited, whose registered office is Fanum House, Basing View, Basingstoke, Hampshire RG21 4EA. Registered number 1878835.

ISBN-10: 0-7495-4834-7
ISBN-13: 978-0-7495-4834-6

English translation © Automobile Association Developments Limited 2006
Translation work by G and W Advertising and Publishing

Cover design by Bookwork Creative Associates, Hampshire
Cover maps © Automobile Association Developments Limited

Colour separation by Kingsclere Design and Print
Printed and bound in China by Leo Paper Products

Cover credits

Front cover : AA World Travel Library/Ken Paterson; **Back cover** : Laurent Parrault

Picture credits

Laurent Parrault : p. 3 (b.r.), 10 (b.r.), 12 (t.l., t.r.), 13 (t.r.), 14, 15 (t.r., c.r.), 16 (t.l., b.c.), 17 (c.r., c.l.), 18 (t.r.), 19 (c.l.), 20 (t.l., b.), 22 (t.l.), 23 (t.r.), 24, 25, 26 (t.l.), 27 (c.c.), 28 (t.l.), 29, 30, 31 (c.l., b.r.), 32, 33, 38 (t.r., c.l.), 39 (b.r.), 40, 41, 43, 44 (b.r.), 45 (b.r.), 47 (t.r., c.c.), 48, 49 (t.l., b.r.), 51, 53 (b.c.), 55 (b.c.), 56, 57 (c.l.), 58 (b.l.), 59 (c.c., b.r.), 60, 61 (b.r.), 62, 63, 67, 69, 71 (t.l.), 73, 74, 75, 78, 79 (t.r.), 82, 83, 90 (t.r., c.r.), 91, 93 (t.r.), 94 (c.l.), 95, 98 (t.l., t.r.), 99, 100, 102, 103, 104, 105, 107 (t.c.), 108 (t.l., b.l.), 109 (t.c., c.r.), 110, 111, 112 (t.r., b.l.), 114, 115, 116 (t.r.), 117 (c.c., b.r.), 118 (t.r., b.c.), 119, 120, 121, 122 (t.l., b.l.), 123 (t.l.), 124, 125 (t.r., b.c.), 126, 130 (c.r.), 132 (t.r.), 137 (t.l.).

Nicolas Edwige : p. 2, 3 (t., c.c., b.l.), 4, 19 (t.r.), 26 (t.r., b.r.), 28 (b.r.), 31 (t.r.), 34, 38 (b.r.), 39 (t.r., c.l., c.c.), 42, 44 (b.l.), 45 (t.l.), 46, 47 (b.r.), 50, 52, 53 (t.c., c.r.), 54, 55 (t.r.), 57 (t.r.), 65, 68, 70, 71 (t.r.), 72, 76, 77, 79 (t.l.), 81, 84, 86 (c.l.), 87 (c.l.), 89 (t.r.), 90 (t.l.), 92, 94 (t.l., t.r.), 96, 98 (b.l.), 101 (t.l.), 106, 107 (c.r.), 108 (t.r.), 112 (t.l.), 113, 116 (t.l., b.c.), 117 (t.l.), 123 (c.c.), 127 (t.c.), 128, 130 (t.l., c.l.), 131, 132 (t.l., c.l.), 135 (t.l., t.r.), 137 (t.r., c.r.).

Christian Sarramon : p. 12 (b.c.), 13 (t.l.), 16 (t.r.), 17 (t.r.), 18 (t.l., b.c.), 19 (b.r.), 20 (t.l.), 22 (t.r., b.c.), 27 (t.l., c.r.), 28 (t.r.), 58 (b.r.), 59 (t.l.), 61 (t.r., c.l.), 66, 118 (t.l.), 122 (t.r., c.r.), 125 (t.l.), 130 (t.r.).

Éric Guillot : p. 127 (c.r.).

Katherine Vanderhaeghe : p. 17 (b.r.).

Hachette : p. 10 (t.r., t.l.), p. 11, 15 (b.c.), 21 (c.l.), 49 (c.r.), 64.

Smokiana : p. 21 (t.r.). **Van Gogh Museum © Jannes Linders** : p. 80 (t.l.). **Van Gogh Museum** : p. 80 (c.l.). **Toro Hotel** : p. 86 (t.r.). **Canal House** : p. 86 (t.l.). **Lloyd Hotel © Rob'Hart** : p. 88, 89 (t.l.). **Ambassade Hotel** : p. 89 (c.c.). **Le Garage** : p. 93 (t.l.). **Zabar's** : p. 93 (c.c.). **Brasserie Harkema** : p. 93 (c.r.). **Van Heek** : p. 101 (c.r.). **Kashba** : p. 109 (c.l.). **De Admiraal** : p. 135 (c.r.).

Illustrations

Pascal Garnier

A02680